Windows Server 2019
Administration Cookbook

Core infrastructure, IIS, Remote Desktop Services,
Monitoring, and Group Policy

Jordan Krause

BIRMINGHAM - MUMBAI

Windows Server 2016 Administration Cookbook

Commissioning Editor: Vijin Boricha
Acquisition Editor: Vinay Argekar
Content Development Editor: Aditi Gour
Technical Editor: Sushmeeta Jena
Copy Editor: Safis Editing
Project Coordinator: Hardik Bhinde
Proofreader: Safis Editing
Indexer: Pratik Shirodkar
Graphics: Jason Monteiro
Production Coordinator: Arvindkumar Gupta

First published: April 2018

Production reference: 1190418

Published by Packt Publishing Ltd.
Livery Place
35 Livery Street
Birmingham
B3 2PB, UK.

ISBN 978-1-78913-593-0

www.packtpub.com

`mapt.io`

Mapt is an online digital library that gives you full access to over 5,000 books and videos, as well as industry leading tools to help you plan your personal development and advance your career. For more information, please visit our website.

Why subscribe?

- Spend less time learning and more time coding with practical eBooks and Videos from over 4,000 industry professionals

- Improve your learning with Skill Plans built especially for you

- Get a free eBook or video every month

- Mapt is fully searchable

- Copy and paste, print, and bookmark content

PacktPub.com

Did you know that Packt offers eBook versions of every book published, with PDF and ePub files available? You can upgrade to the eBook version at `www.PacktPub.com` and as a print book customer, you are entitled to a discount on the eBook copy. Get in touch with us at `service@packtpub.com` for more details.

At `www.PacktPub.com`, you can also read a collection of free technical articles, sign up for a range of free newsletters, and receive exclusive discounts and offers on Packt books and eBooks.

Contributors

About the author

Jordan Krause is a six-time Microsoft MVP, currently awarded in the Cloud and Datacenter Management category. He has the unique opportunity to work daily with the Microsoft networking and remote access technologies as a Senior Engineer at IVO Networks. Jordan specializes in Microsoft DirectAccess and Always On VPN. Committed to continuous learning, Jordan holds certifications as an MCP, MCTS, MCSA, and MCITP Enterprise Administrator, and regularly writes articles reflecting his experiences with these technologies. Jordan lives and works in beautiful west Michigan (USA).

About the reviewer

Florian Klaffenbach is a solutions architect and consultant for Microsoft Infrastructure and cloud, specialized in Microsoft Hyper-V, Fileservices, System Center Virtual Machine Manager, and Microsoft Azure IaaS. He is also a cochairman of the Azure Community Germany. In April 2016, Microsoft awarded Florian the Microsoft Most Valued Professional for Cloud and Datacenter Management. Currently, he is working at MSG service AG as a senior consultant of Microsoft cloud infrastructure.

He has also worked on many books by Packt Publishing.

Packt is searching for authors like you

If you're interested in becoming an author for Packt, please visit authors.packtpub.com and apply today. We have worked with thousands of developers and tech professionals, just like you, to help them share their insight with the global tech community. You can make a general application, apply for a specific hot topic that we are recruiting an author for, or submit your own idea.

Table of Contents

Preface

Microsoft is the clear leader of server racks in enterprise data centers across the globe. Walk into any backroom or data center of any company and you are almost guaranteed to find the infrastructure of that organization being supported by the Windows Server operating system. We have been relying on Windows Server for more than 20 years, and rightfully so--nowhere else can you find such an enormous mix of capabilities all provided inside one installer disc. Windows Server 2016 continues to provide the core functionality that we have come to rely upon from all previous versions of Windows Server, but in better and more efficient ways. On top of that, we have some brand new capabilities in Server 2016 that are particularly mind-bending, new ways to accomplish more efficient and secure handling of our network traffic and data.

There is a relevant question mixed into all this server talk, "We hear so much about the cloud. Isn't everyone moving to the cloud? If so, why would we even need Windows Server 2016 in our company?" There are two different ways to answer this question, and both result in having huge benefits to knowing and understanding this newest version of Windows Server. First, there really aren't that many companies moving **all** of their equipment into the cloud. In fact, I have yet to meet any business with more than 10 employees who has gone all-in for the cloud. In almost all cases, it still makes sense that you would use at least one on premise server to manage local user account authentication, or DHCP, or print services, or for a local file server—the list goes on and on. Another reason companies aren't moving to the cloud like you might think they are is security. Sure, we might throw some data and some user accounts to the cloud to enable things like federation and ease of accessing that data, but what about sensitive or classified company data? You don't own your data if it resides in the cloud – you don't even have the capability to manage the backend servers that are actually storing that data alongside data from other companies. How can you be guaranteed of your data's security and survival? The ultimate answer is that you cannot, though there are steps being made in this direction. This alone keeps many folks that I have talked to away from moving some of their information to a cloud service provider.

The second reason it is still important to build knowledge on the Windows Server platform is that even if you have made the decision to move everything to the cloud, what server platform will you be running in the cloud that you now have to log into and administer? If you are using Azure for cloud services, there is a very good chance that you will be logging into Windows Server 2016 instances in order to administer your environment, even if those Server 2016 boxes are sitting in the cloud. So whether you have on premise servers, or you are managing servers sitting in the cloud somewhere, learning all you can about the new Windows Server 2016 operating system will be beneficial to your day job in IT.

When I first learned of the opportunity to put together this book, it was a difficult task to assemble an outline of possible recipes. Where to begin? There are so many different roles that can be run in Windows Server 2016, and so many tasks within each role that could be displayed. It was a natural reaction to start looking for all of the things that are brand new in Server 2016, and to want to talk only about recipes that display the latest and greatest features. But then I realized that those recipes on their own won't accomplish anything helpful for someone who is trying to learn about Windows Server administration for the first time. It is critical that we provide a base understanding of the important infrastructural roles that are commonly provided by Windows Server, because without that baseline the newest features won't amount to a hill of beans.

This shortened volume focuses more on the common, everyday recipes that are going to benefit the average server administrator, and I hope that this book can also be a quick-reference guide that you keep near your desk into the future until you are fully versed and comfortable navigating around the new interface. We will cover recipes that tackle the core infrastructure tasks that we have been performing in previous versions of Windows Server, but now focusing on how to make them work in the new Windows Server 2016. Some recipes are clearly for the beginner, while others get deeper into the details so that someone already experienced with working inside Windows Server will gain some new knowledge out of reading this book. We will discuss the roles that are critically important to making any Microsoft network function: Active Directory, DNS, DHCP, Group Policy and so on.

A primary goal of this cookbook is to be a reference guide that you can come back to time and again when you need to accomplish common tasks in your environment, but want to ensure that you are performing them the right way. I hope that through these chapters you are able to become comfortable enough with Windows Server 2016 that you will go out and install it today!

Who this book is for

This book is for system administrators and IT professionals that may or may not have previous experience with Windows Server 2012 R2 or its predecessors. Since the start of this book, I have been contacted and asked many times whether the core, baseline information to beginning to work with Windows Server will be included. These requests have come from current desktop administrators wanting to get into the server world, and even from developers hoping to better understand the infrastructure upon which their applications run. Both will benefit from the information provided here. Anyone hoping to acquire the skills and knowledge necessary to manage and maintain the core infrastructure required for a Windows Server 2016 environment should find something interesting on the pages contained within.

What this book covers

Chapter 1, *Learning the Interface,* starts us on our journey working with Windows Server 2016 as we figure out how to navigate the look and feel of this new operating system, and gain some tips and tricks to make our daily chores more efficient.

Chapter 2, *Core Infrastructure Tasks,* takes us through configuring and working with the core Microsoft technology stack. The recipes contained in this chapter are what I consider essential knowledge for any administrator who intends to work in a Windows network.

Chapter 3, *Internet Information Services,* brings us into the configuration of a Windows Server 2016 box as a web server in our network. Strangely, in the field I find a lot of Microsoft networks with Apache web servers floating around that nobody likes to administer. Let's explore IIS as a better and more secure alternative.

Chapter 4, *Remote Desktop Services,* encourages you to look into using Server 2016 as a virtual session host or VDI solution. RDS can be an incredibly powerful tool for anyone interested in centralized computing.

Chapter 5, *Monitoring and Backup,* covers some of the capabilities included with Server 2016 to help keep tabs on the servers running in your infrastructure. From monitoring system performance and IP address management to backing up and restoring data using the tools baked into Windows, these recipes will walk you through some helpful tasks related to monitoring and backup.

Chapter 6, *Group Policy,* takes us into the incredibly powerful and far reaching management powers contained within Active Directory that are provided out of the box with Windows Server 2016.

To get the most out of this book

All the technologies and features that are discussed in the recipes of this book are included with Windows Server 2016. As long as you have access to the operating system installer disc and either a piece of hardware or a virtualization environment where you can spin up a new virtual machine, you will be able to install the operating system and follow along with our lessons.

Many of the tasks that we are going to accomplish together require a certain amount of base networking and infrastructure to be configured, in order to fully test the technologies that we are working with. The easiest method to working through all of these recipes will be to have access to a Hyper-V server upon which you can build multiple virtual machines that run Windows Server 2016. With this available, you will be able to build recipe upon recipe as we move through setting up the core infrastructural tasks, and then utilize those same servers to build upon in the later recipes. Building a baseline lab network running Server 2016 for the Microsoft infrastructure roles like Active Directory, DNS, and DHCP will help you tremendously as you move throughout this book and your job in IT. If you are not familiar with building out a lab, do not be dismayed. Many of the recipes included here will help with building the structure of the lab itself.

Download the color images

We also provide a PDF file that has color images of the screenshots/diagrams used in this book. You can download it here: `http://www.packtpub.com/sites/default/files/downloads/WindowsServer2016AdministrationCookbook_ColorImages.pdf`.

Conventions used

There are a number of text conventions used throughout this book.

`CodeInText`: Indicates code words in text, database table names, folder names, filenames, file extensions, pathnames, dummy URLs, user input, and Twitter handles. Here is an example: "Mount the downloaded `WebStorm-10*.dmg` disk image file as another disk in your system."

A block of code is set as follows:

```
html, body, #map {
 height: 100%;
 margin: 0;
 padding: 0
}
```

When we wish to draw your attention to a particular part of a code block, the relevant lines or items are set in bold:

```
[default]
exten => s,1,Dial(Zap/1|30)
exten => s,2,Voicemail(u100)
exten => s,102,Voicemail(b100)
exten => i,1,Voicemail(s0)
```

Any command-line input or output is written as follows:

```
$ mkdir css
$ cd css
```

Bold: Indicates a new term, an important word, or words that you see onscreen. For example, words in menus or dialog boxes appear in the text like this. Here is an example: "Select **System info** from the **Administration** panel."

Warnings or important notes appear like this.

Tips and tricks appear like this.

Get in touch

Feedback from our readers is always welcome.

General feedback: Email feedback@packtpub.com and mention the book title in the subject of your message. If you have questions about any aspect of this book, please email us at questions@packtpub.com.

Errata: Although we have taken every care to ensure the accuracy of our content, mistakes do happen. If you have found a mistake in this book, we would be grateful if you would report this to us. Please visit www.packtpub.com/submit-errata, selecting your book, clicking on the Errata Submission Form link, and entering the details.

Piracy: If you come across any illegal copies of our works in any form on the Internet, we would be grateful if you would provide us with the location address or website name. Please contact us at copyright@packtpub.com with a link to the material.

If you are interested in becoming an author: If there is a topic that you have expertise in and you are interested in either writing or contributing to a book, please visit authors.packtpub.com.

Reviews

Please leave a review. Once you have read and used this book, why not leave a review on the site that you purchased it from? Potential readers can then see and use your unbiased opinion to make purchase decisions, we at Packt can understand what you think about our products, and our authors can see your feedback on their book. Thank you!

For more information about Packt, please visit packtpub.com.

Bibliography

The material in the book has been selected from the content of Packt's **Windows Server 2016 Cookbook** by Jordan Krause to provide a specific focus on key Windows Server administration tasks.

Learning the Interface 1

In an effort to become familiar with the look and feel of Windows Server 2016, you will learn how to navigate through some daily tasks using the graphical interface. On our agenda in this chapter are the following recipes:

- Shutting down or restarting the server
- Launching Administrative Tools
- Using WinKey + X for quick admin tasks
- Using the search function to launch applications quickly
- Managing remote servers from a single pane with Server Manager
- Using PowerShell to accomplish any function in Windows Server
- Installing a role or feature
- Administering Server 2016 from a Windows 10 machine
- Identifying useful keyboard shortcuts in Server 2016
- Setting your PowerShell Execution Policy
- Building and executing your first PowerShell script
- Searching for PowerShell cmdlets with Get-Help

Introduction

Windows 8 and Server 2012 brought us a drastic change in the way that we interfaced with the Windows operating system, and most of us didn't think that change was for the better. By now I assume you have all seen, used, and are hopefully deploying Windows 10 on your client computers, which brings some relief with regard to the user interface. With Windows 10 we have kind of a mix between Windows 7 and Windows 8, and it fits the needs of most people in a better way. Just like the last couple of rollouts of the Microsoft Windows operating systems, the Server platform follows on the heels of the Desktop version, and the look and feel of Windows Server 2016 is very much like Windows 10. In fact, I would say that Windows 10 and Windows Server 2016 are more alike than the Windows 7/Server 2008 combination or the Windows 8/Server 2012 combination.

If you have been using Windows 10, you already have a good head start for successfully interfacing with Windows Server 2016. However, if you are still using older equipment and haven't had a chance to really dive into the latest and greatest operating systems, these big changes in the way that we interact with our servers can be a big stumbling block to successfully utilizing the new tools. Many differences exist when comparing Server 2016 to something like Server 2008, and when you are working within three levels of **Remote Desktop Protocol (RDP)**, bouncing from one server to another, all of these little differences are compounded. It suddenly becomes difficult to know which server it is that you are working on or changing. Let's have a show of hands, how many of you have mistakenly rebooted the wrong server? Or even more likely, how many of you have rebooted your own computer while you were trying to reboot a remote server? I know I have! And not just once.

Hope is not lost! I promise you that, once you learn to manage the interface, rather than letting it manage you, some of these changes may start to seem like good ideas. They can increase productivity and the ease of accomplishing tasks—we just need some pointers on making the best use of the new interface.

The recipes in this chapter are dedicated to doing just that. Let's work together to gain a better understanding of why the interface was built the way it is, and learn to take advantage of these new screens and settings.

Shutting down or restarting the server

I just couldn't resist starting with this one. Yes, this seems trivial. Silly even. However, the number of times that I have watched a simple server restart consume more mouse clicks than creating a domain controller has convinced me that this needed to be in the book. Perhaps the shutdown and restart options were hidden away purposefully because once your system is up and running, there is not often a need to accomplish either of these tasks. When first configuring the box, though, it is very common to have to reboot a couple of time or to shut down a machine to move it to another location. Let's face it, it doesn't seem to matter how many years computers have been around, many times the magical reboot is still the fix—all answer to most problems, even if we have no idea why.

Getting ready

To go through this recipe, you will need a Windows Server 2016 system online. There are no other prerequisites.

How to do it...

Let's take a look at three different ways to shut down or restart your system. The first is going to be the most commonly employed. The second is still being used by quite a few folks who had to work hard at getting this strange location in their heads during the Windows 8 rollout, and they have continued to use it from that point forward. The third is less commonly known but is by far my favorite when tasked with restarting a remote server.

The first option, thankfully, is in a location that actually makes sense. I say thankfully because when Server 2012 was released, this option didn't exist, and finding the restart function was much more difficult. Just like we have always been able to do prior to the Windows 8 rollout, we can simply click on the *Start* button and see right there near the bottom that we have *Power* control options available to us:

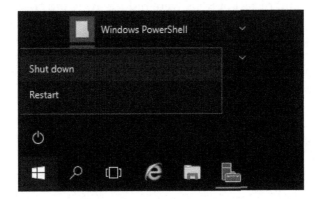

Now, when you click on **Shut down** or **Restart**, you are asked to supply a reason why you are restarting. Common sense tells us that if you are manually clicking on the **Restart** button, there is a pretty good chance you are actually intending to restart the server, right? A planned occurrence? But what is the default option that presents itself? **Other (Unplanned)**. Alas, this silly default option is certainly going to cause us log files full of unplanned restarts, even though all of those restarts were actually planned. Because let's be real—nobody takes the time to change that drop-down menu before they click **Continue**:

The second method to accomplish shutting down or restarting is by right-clicking on the Start button. We will discuss this little menu that is presented when right-clicking on *Start* in our next recipe, but for the sake of a quick shut down or restart, you can simply right-click on the *Start* button, and then choose **Shut down or sign out**:

Each of the previous two examples runs the risk of rebooting the wrong system. Depending on how many layers of remote connections, such as RDP, you are using, it is fairly easy to reboot your own computer or the wrong server instead of the server you intended to reboot, because it is fairly easy to click on the *Start* button of a different system than the one you intended in the first place. The most definitive, and dare I say the most fun way of restarting your server is to utilize a Command Prompt. Doing this gives you the opportunity to double check that you are manipulating the correct machine. Open up a Command Prompt and run a quick hostname check to make sure you are restarting the one you really intend to. Then utilize the shutdown command to take care of the rest. This process can be especially helpful when logged into remote servers using RDP. Use the following commands to perform the explained operations:

```
hostname
shutdown /r /t 0
```

If you were to simply type shutdown, the server would shut itself down in 60 seconds. Using /r indicates a restart rather than a shutdown, and /t 0 is a timing flag that indicates the number of seconds the server should wait before restarting. Specifying slash zero here tells it to wait for zero seconds before initiating the restart:

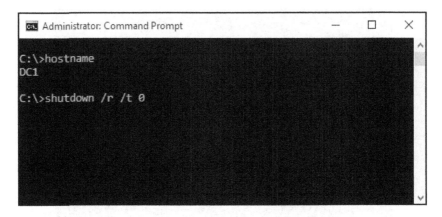

How it works...

Shutting down or restarting a server doesn't require a lot of explanation, but I hope that this small recipe gets some thought going about creative ways to do regular tasks. As you will see throughout this book, you can accomplish anything in Windows Server 2016 through the use of commands or scripts. You could easily turn the shutdown command, the last example that we tested in this recipe, into a batch file, and place it on the Desktop of each of your servers as a quick double-click option for accomplishing this task.

However, I work with RDP windows inside RDP windows very often. When you're bouncing around between a dozen servers that all have the same background image, I have decided that the only sure-fire way to make sure you are restarting the correct device is to do a quick hostname check before you initiate the restart. If you are interested in discovering all of the available flags that are available to use with the shutdown command, make sure to type in shutdown /? some time to take a look at all of the available options.

Using the Command Prompt is also an easy way to log off a server. Let's say you are layers-deep in RDP and want to log off from a single server (not all of them). Are you sure you clicked on the *Start* button of the right server? Instead, open up a prompt and simply type Logoff.

Launching Administrative Tools

Earlier versions of Windows Server placed all of the Administrative Tools in a self-named folder right inside the *Start* menu. This was always a quick and easy place to visit in order to see all of the Administrative Tools installed on a particular server. This location for the tools disappeared as of Server 2012, because of the infamous Start Screen. I am glad to say that a more traditional-looking *Start* menu has returned in Windows Server 2016, and inside it once again is a link to the **Windows Administrative Tools**. However, as you also know there is this thing called **Server Manager** that loves to present itself every time that you log in to a server. Since **Server Manager** is already on your screen most of the time anyway, it is actually the fastest way to launch these Administrative Tools that you need to utilize so often. Let's take a look at launching your commonly used infrastructure tools right from inside the **Server Manager** interface.

Getting ready

All you really need is a Windows Server 2016 machine online. The more roles and services that you have running on it, the more options that you will see on your screen as we navigate these menus.

How to do it...

To launch Administrative Tools from your Desktop, perform the following steps:

1. Open up **Server Manager**. In fact, if you just logged into the server, it's probably already open for you.
2. Click on **Tools** in the upper-right corner.

There you go. A full list of all the Administrative Tools installed onto that server. Heading into this list is also a quick way of taking a look at what a particular server is doing, which you can take an educated guess at based on what roles and services are installed. By looking at the following screenshot, we can see that this server appears to be a domain controller that is also running DNS and DHCP, because all of the related tools are available to choose in this list. That is accurate, as this is my DC1 domain controller server. It is important to note that your server may be running components that do not show up in this list. For example, if you install a role via PowerShell and do not enter the parameter to also install the management tools for that role, it is possible that you could have a server where the role is up and running, but the management tools simply have not been installed. In that case, those tools would not show up in this list:

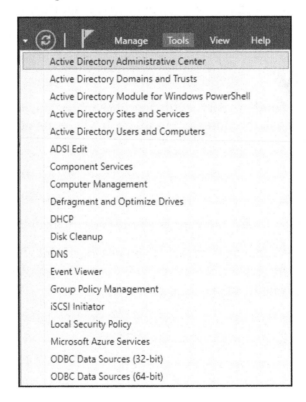

How it works...

Since Server Manager likes to open automatically when logging in, let's make quick use of it to open the tools that we need to do our jobs. Another way to have easy access to your tools from the desktop is to create shortcuts or to pin each of them to your taskbar. Sometimes this isn't as easy as it sounds. In the past, these tools were all grouped together in the `Administrative Tools` folder, so you didn't have any reason to memorize the exact names of the tools. While you can access them that way again in Server 2016, that folder may or may not appear inside the Start menu depending on how the server is configured, because it appears as one of the live tiles. If you click on the *Start* button, you could try using the search function to find the tool you are looking for, but its name may not immediately come to you. If you're a consultant working on someone else's server, you may not want to pin anything to their desktop anyway, and you certainly don't want to resort to using Bing in front of them to look up the name of the tool. So I like to stick with launching Administrative Tools from **Server Manager** since it always exists, and the tools will always be available inside that menu.

Using WinKey + X for quick admin tasks

There are some functions in Windows that a server administrator needs to use all the time. Instead of making shortcuts or pinning them all to the taskbar, let's get to know this hidden menu, which is extremely useful for launching these commonly used admin tools.

Getting ready

A running Windows Server 2016 machine is all we need to highlight this one. In fact, this menu also exists on any Windows 10 computer, so make use of it often!

How to do it...

There are two ways to open this little menu. While you are on the Server 2016 desktop, you can perform either of these steps:

1. Hold down your *Windows key (WinKey)* on the keyboard and press *X*

2. Hover your mouse over the Windows flag in the lower-left corner of the desktop—the start button—when you right-click on that button you will see a menu, shown in the following screenshot:

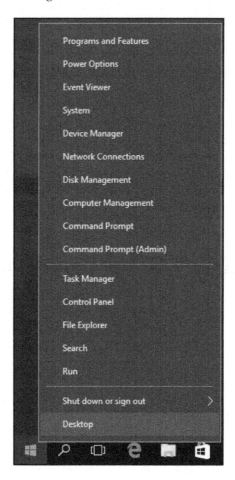

How it works...

This little quick-tasks admin menu is very easy to open and is very convenient for launching programs and settings that are accessed often. I won't talk too much about what particulars are in the menu as it's pretty self-explanatory, but I use this menu multiple times per day to open up the **System** properties and the **Command Prompt**, as it has an option to open an administrative Command Prompt right from the menu.

Look at that, you can also shut down the server from here!

Using the search function to launch applications quickly

The *Start* screen in Windows Server 2012 was not the greatest idea to come out of Microsoft, and unfortunately what it did was train people to no longer click on the *Start* button, so that we didn't have to deal with the Start screen. Windows 10, and therefore Windows Server 2016, have moved back to a more traditional Start menu, but it is going to take a little bit of time to retrain ourselves to make use of it on a daily basis. I know it will for myself, anyway. Ever since Windows 7 was released, I have been using the Start menu for one critical function in my daily workflow: searching. Let's explore the search capabilities of Server 2016, which can be accessed with a single press of a button.

Getting ready

For this recipe, you will need a Windows Server 2016 system online.

How to do it...

There are two quick ways that you can search inside Server 2016, and they are right next to each other. If you take a look in the lower-left corner of your screen inside the taskbar, you will see a little magnifying glass next to the Start button. Looks like a search function to me. Click on that button, and you can start typing the name of whatever you would like to search for. In the following screenshot, you can see that I have clicked on my magnifying glass and typed cmd in order to find the **Command Prompt** application:

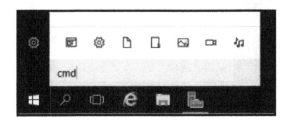

Search results are presented at the top of that screen, and you can choose what you are looking for accordingly. This is a quick, easy search—but I'm not a fan of it because I don't like using my mouse unless I have to. Grabbing my mouse in order to click on the magnifying glass slows down what I'm trying to do while my hands are on the keyboard, so let's take a look at a faster way to search. No matter where you are in Windows Server 2016, no matter what applications you have open, you can always press the *WinKey* on your keyboard to open up the Start menu, right? What you may not know is that as soon as your Start menu is open, you can immediately start typing anything in order to search for it. If you need to open **Command Prompt**, press *WinKey* and type cmd. If you need to search for a document called Text1, press *WinKey* and type Text1. I employ this method of opening applications all day every day. This way I don't have to pin anything, I don't have to create any shortcuts, and most importantly, I don't have to use my mouse in order to launch applications:

How it works...

From the Start menu, we can search for anything on the server. This gives us the ability to quickly find and launch any program or application that we have installed. This includes **Administrative Tools**. Rather than moving into **Server Manager** in order to launch your administrative consoles from the **Tools** menu, you can also search for them on the **Search** menu, and launch from there. It also gives us the ability to find files or documents by name. Another powerful way to use the search function in Windows Server 2016 is to open any kind of setting that you might want to change. In previous versions of Windows, you had to either memorize the way to get into the settings that you wanted to change or you had to open up **Control Panel**, where you had to poke and prod your way around until you stumbled upon the one that you were looking for. Now it is a very simple matter of pressing the Windows key, typing the first few characters of the setting or program you want to launch, and pressing *Enter*.

Another common task to perform from the **Search** screen is to right-click on the application that you are trying to launch and pin it somewhere. When you right-click on a program from the **Search** screen, you see options to pin the program to either your **Start** menu or to the taskbar. This will create a quick-launch shortcut on either the main **Start** menu or on the taskbar of the desktop mode, giving you easier and faster access to launch those applications in the future.

Managing remote servers from a single pane with Server Manager

As you have already noticed, **Server Manager** has changed significantly over the past couple of versions of Windows Server. Part of these changes is a shift in mindset where the emphasis is now placed on remote management of servers. **Server Manager** in Windows Server 2016 can be used to manage and administer multiple systems at the same time, all from your single pane of glass, the monitor where you are sitting. In this recipe, you are going to learn how to manage both the local server we are logged into, as well as a remote server, from the same Server Manager window.

Getting ready

For this recipe, we need two servers. One is the machine we are physically logged into. Another is a server on the same network that we can contact from our primary server so that we can manage it from our local **Server Manager**.

How to do it...

To manage a local as well as a remote server from the same **Server Manager** window, perform the following instructions:

1. Log in to your primary server and launch **Server Manager**. You will see in the upper-left corner that the only server you have listed is the **Local Server** that we are logged into:

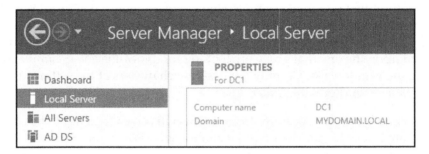

2. Now head over toward the top-right of **Server Manager** and click on the **Manage** button. In this menu, click on **Add Servers** as shown in the following screenshot:

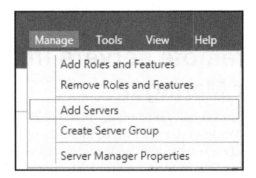

3. If your servers are part of a domain, finding remote machines to manage is very easy by simply selecting them from the default **Active Directory** tab. If they are not yet joined to your domain, you simply click over to the tab labeled **DNS** and search for them from that screen:

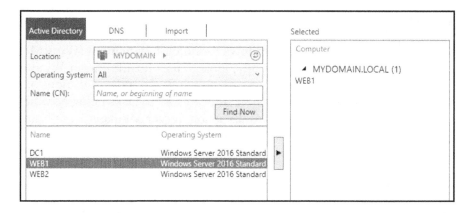

4. After adding the servers that you want to manage, if you go ahead and click on **All Servers** in the left window pane, you will see the additional servers listed that you have selected. If you double-click or right-click on those remote server names, you have many options available to you to remotely manage those machines without having to log into them:

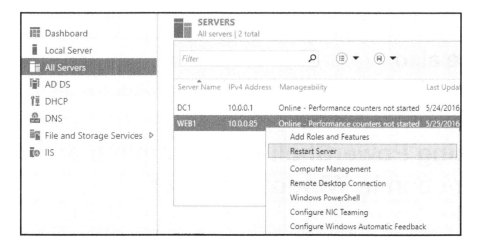

Note that certain servers could resist being manipulated in this way. It is possible to restrict remote management on servers through Group Policy. If that has been done in your environment, you may find that remotely administering them from a centralized console is not possible, and you would have to lift those restrictions on your servers.

How it works...

Server Manager makes use of the **Windows Remote Management (WinRM)** tools to remotely manipulate servers. Historically, most of us who administer Windows Servers make extensive use of RDP, often having many windows and connections open simultaneously. This can cause confusion and can lead to tasks being accomplished on servers for which they are not intended. By using **Server Manager** from a single machine to manage multiple servers in your network, you will increase your administrative efficiency as well as minimize human error by having all management happen from a single pane of glass.

This recipe is written with the most common network scenario in mind, which is a domain environment where both servers have been joined to the domain. If you are working with standalone servers that are part of a workgroup, rather than being joined to a domain, you will have some additional considerations. In the workgroup scenario, WinRM will need to be enabled specifically, and the Windows Firewall will have to be adjusted in order to allow the right ports and protocols for that WinRM traffic flow to happen successfully. In general, though, most of you will be working within a Microsoft domain network, in which case these items are not necessary.

See also

- The *Administering Server 2016 from a Windows 10 machine* recipe

Using PowerShell to accomplish any function in Windows Server

An incredibly powerful tool in Windows Server 2016 is PowerShell. Think of PowerShell like a Command Prompt on steroids. It is a command-line interface from which you can manipulate almost anything inside Windows that you may care to. Better yet, any task that you may wish to accomplish can be scripted out in PowerShell and saved off as a .ps1 script file, so that you can automate large tasks and schedule them for later, or at regular intervals. In this recipe, let's open up PowerShell and run some sample commands and tasks just to get a quick feel for the interface. In a later chapter of the book, we will do some more specific tasks with PowerShell to go even deeper into the technology.

Getting ready

To start using PowerShell, all you need is a server with Windows Server 2016 installed. PowerShell is installed and enabled by default.

How to do it...

To get a feel of using PowerShell, perform the following steps:

1. PowerShell used to exist in the taskbar by default, which was smart because we really should be pushing people to use it rather than **Command Prompt**, right? Unfortunately, PowerShell is not in the taskbar by default in Server 2016, but the Windows Store is...? Explain that one to me some day. So our first step to working in PowerShell is finding it. Thankfully, we know how to search for applications now, so I'll just press my *WinKey* and type PowerShell. Once my search result is displayed, I am going to right-click on **Windows PowerShell** and choose to **Run as administrator**:

2. Test out some commands that you are familiar with from using the Command Prompt, such as dir and cls. Since you are able to make use of these familiar commands, PowerShell can really be your one and only command-line interface if you choose.

3. Now let's try some of the PowerShell secret sauce, one of its cmdlets. These are special commands that are built into Windows and allow us to do all kinds of information gathering, as well as manipulation of server components. Let's start by pulling some data. Maybe take a look at what IP addresses are on the system with `Get-NetIPAddress`:

```
Administrator: Windows PowerShell                                    —    □    ×
PS C:\> Get-NetIPAddress


IPAddress              : fe80::79a1:f04f:406e:f589%2
ValidLifetime          : Infinite ([TimeSpan]::MaxValue)
PreferredLifetime      : Infinite ([TimeSpan]::MaxValue)
SkipAsSource           : False
PolicyStore            : ActiveStore

IPAddress              : fe80::5efe:10.0.0.85%4
InterfaceIndex         : 4
InterfaceAlias         : isatap.MYDOMAIN.LOCAL
AddressFamily          : IPv6
Type                   : Unicast
PrefixLength           : 128
PolicyStore            : ActiveStore
```

4. The previous command probably gave you a lot more information than you needed, since most companies don't make use of `IPv6` inside their network yet. Let's whittle this information down to the `IPv4`-specific info that you are most likely interested in. Enter `Get-NetIPAddress -AddressFamily IPv4` to attain it:

```
Administrator: Windows PowerShell                                    —    □    ×
PS C:\> Get-NetIPAddress -AddressFamily IPv4


IPAddress              : 10.0.0.85
InterfaceIndex         : 2
InterfaceAlias         : Ethernet
AddressFamily          : IPv4
Type                   : Unicast
PrefixLength           : 24
PrefixOrigin           : Dhcp
SuffixOrigin           : Dhcp
AddressState           : Preferred
ValidLifetime          : 5.23:17:10
PreferredLifetime      : 5.23:17:10
SkipAsSource           : False
PolicyStore            : ActiveStore
```

How it works...

PowerShell has so many commands and cmdlets, we just wanted to get a feel for launching the program and pulling some data with this particular recipe. There are countless `Get` commands to query information from the server, and as you have seen those cmdlets have various parameters that can be appended to the cmdlets to pull more specific data to meet your needs. To make things even better, there are not only `Get` cmdlets, but also `Set` cmdlets, which will allow us to make use of the PowerShell prompt to configure many aspects of the configuration on our server, as well as remote servers. We will dive further into PowerShell in a later chapter.

Installing a role or feature

You've installed the Windows Server 2016 operating system onto a piece of hardware. Great! Now what? Without adding roles and features to your server, it makes a great paperweight. We're going to take the next steps here together. Let's install a role and a feature into Windows so that we can start making this server work for us.

Getting ready

As long as you have a Windows Server 2016 installed and running, you are ready to install roles and features onto that machine.

How to do it...

To install a role and a feature into Windows, perform the following steps:

1. Open **Server Manager**. In the middle of the screen, you'll see a link that says **Add roles and features**. Click on that link.

2. Click **Next** on the first summary screen and you will come to a choice on the second page. For most roles and features, we want to leave it set at the top bullet, which is **Role-based or feature-based installation**. If we were Configuring Remote Desktop Services, which we will discuss in another chapter, then we would choose the second option.

3. Now we choose where we want to install a new role or feature. This is a neat page, as we can choose from any server that we have added into our **Server Manager**, or we can even choose to install a role or feature into a virtual hard disk. I am running the **Add Roles Wizard** from DC1, but I want to install the IIS role onto WEB1. Rather than having to log into WEB1 to accomplish this task, I will do it right from here. In the following screenshot, you can see WEB1 listed as a server that I can install a role onto, even though I am opening this console on the DC1 server:

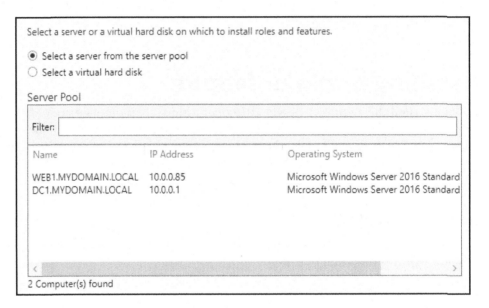

Select a server or a virtual hard disk on which to install roles and features.

◉ Select a server from the server pool
○ Select a virtual hard disk

Server Pool

Filter:

Name	IP Address	Operating System
WEB1.MYDOMAIN.LOCAL	10.0.0.85	Microsoft Windows Server 2016 Standard
DC1.MYDOMAIN.LOCAL	10.0.0.1	Microsoft Windows Server 2016 Standard

2 Computer(s) found

4. Scroll down and choose the role that you want to install. For WEB1, I am choosing the **Web Server (IIS)** role. Then click **Next**.

You can install more than one role or feature at a time. Some roles require additional components to be installed for them to work properly. For example, when I chose to install the IIS role and clicked **Next**, I was prompted about needing to install some management tools. Simply click on the **Add Features** button to automatically add the items that it needs to perform correctly.

5. Now choose any features that you would like to install. For example, in order to do some network connectivity testing later, go ahead and select **Telnet Client** from the list.

6. Read and click **Next** through the informational messages that are displayed. These messages will vary depending on which roles and features you have installed.

7. The final screen is your installation summary. If everything looks correct, go ahead and click on **Install**.

After your roles and features have finished installing, the server may or may not have to reboot. This depends on whether or not the role installation requires it. Following installation, or following the reboot, if your new role needs any additional configuration or setting up to be completed, you will be notified at the top of the Server Manager screen.

How it works...

Adding roles and features to a Windows Server is something that every administrator will have to do sooner or later. These items are necessary to turn on the functions in the server that will perform tasks that need to be performed in your environment. Adding roles is quite straightforward. However, it is interesting to see the options that are available to add more than one role or feature at a time. Moreover, the ability to remotely install these items for servers in your network that you are not logged into is intriguing.

Administering Server 2016 from a Windows 10 machine

In the *Managing remote servers from a single pane with Server Manager* recipe, we discussed remotely administering another server by using Server Manager. Did you know we can accomplish the same remote management by using our day-to-day Windows 10 computer? We will install and use the **Remote Server Administration Tools** (**RSAT**) to take even more advantage of Server 2016's remote management ideology.

Getting ready

To test out the RSAT tools, we will need a Windows 10 client machine. We will then also need a Windows Server 2016 system online, and on the same network, which we can remotely control and manage.

How to do it...

To remotely manage a server using RSAT, follow these instructions:

1. First, we need to download the RSAT tools. You can use Bing to search for Remote Server Administration Tools for Windows 10, or use this link to download RSAT for Windows 10: `https://www.microsoft.com/en-us/download/details.aspx?id=45520`. Here is also the link for the same RSAT tools in the Windows 8.1 flavor: `http://www.microsoft.com/en-us/download/details.aspx?id=39296`. After you install these tools onto your Windows 10 or 8.1 computer, you should now have a copy of Server Manager installed onto your computer. Go ahead and launch that from the Start menu. You can pin it to your Taskbar for quicker launching in the future, of course. In the same fashion, as with Server 2016, you can use the **Manage** menu to add servers to Server Manager:

2. For this recipe, I do have the machines we are working with joined to a domain, so we will take a look at adding servers that are part of the domain.
3. Click on the **Find Now** button and you will see a list of server names that are remotely manageable:

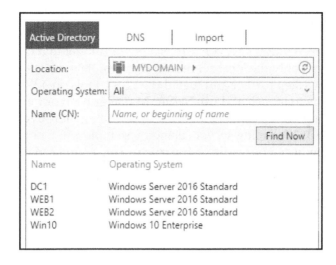

4. Click on the server names that you want to administer and click on the arrow to move them over to the right side of the screen. Upon clicking on **OK**, you will see these new servers listed and ready for management inside your **Server Manager** console:

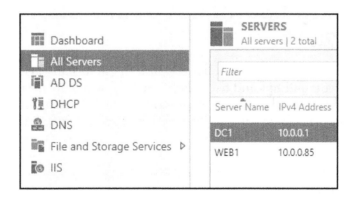

How it works...

Server Manager in Windows Server 2016 is a powerful tool that can be used for the management of not only the local server but also remote servers that you want to manage. If we take this even a step further and install the RSAT tools on a Windows 10 computer, this gives us the ability to launch and use **Server Manager** from our everyday Windows 10 computer. In doing so, we enable ourselves to add roles, view events, and restart servers, all from our own desk. Managing servers using these tools will increase productivity and decrease errors because your entire infrastructure of servers can be available within a single window. This is much more efficient than using the RDP client to connect to many different servers, all in different windows. If you've never tried using RSAT to manage servers, give it a try!

See also

- The *Managing remote servers from a single pane with Server Manager* recipe

Identifying useful keyboard shortcuts in Server 2016

I prefer using a keyboard over a mouse any day, for almost any task. There are numerous keyboard shortcuts and tips and tricks that I employ on a daily basis and I want to test them out with you in this recipe. Some of these shortcuts have been around for years and will work with multiple versions of Windows Server; some are new in the Server 2016 operating system. They will all be useful to you as you start working with servers in your network.

Getting ready

We are going to run these commands and keyboard shortcuts while logged into a Windows Server 2016 machine.

How to do it...

- *Windows* key: Opens the **Start** menu, where you can immediately start typing to search for programs.

- *Windows key + X*: Opens the Quick Links menu, which we discussed in an earlier recipe.
- *Windows key + I*: Opens Windows **Settings** options.
- *Windows key + D*: Minimizes all open windows and brings you back to the Desktop.
- *Windows key + R*: Opens the **Run** box. Launching applications this way is often faster than using the Start menu, if you know the executable name of the application you are trying to launch.
- *Windows key + M*: Minimizes all windows.
- *Windows key + E*: Opens File Explorer.
- *Windows key + L*: Locks the computer.
- *Windows key + Tab*: Takes you into the new Task View options.
- *Window key + Ctrl + D*: Creates a new virtual Desktop from Task View.
- *Windows key + Ctrl + F4*: Closes the current virtual Desktop.
- *Windows key + Ctrl + Left or Right Arrow*: Move between different virtual Desktops.
- *Windows key + 1 or 2 or 3 or...*: Launches applications that are pinned to your taskbar, in order. So the first application pinned to the taskbar would open with WinKey + 1, for example.
- *Alt + F4*: Exits the program you are currently working in. This is especially helpful in full-screen apps—like those from the Windows Store - where it is not always obvious how to exit the program with your mouse.
- *Alt + Tab*: Displays a list of open programs so you can hop between them.
- *Shift + Delete*: Holding down *Shift* while pressing *Delete* deletes files without placing them into the Recycle Bin.
- Using *Tab* inside Command Prompt or PowerShell: I cannot believe that I went years without knowing about this one. When you are working inside Command Prompt, if you type the first letter of a file or folder that exists in the directory where you are working and then press the *Tab* key, it will auto-populate the rest of the filename. For example, you may be trying to launch a Microsoft update file with a filename that is 15 characters and comprises a mix of numbers and letters. No need to type out that filename! Let's say the file starts with KB. Simply navigate to the folder where your installer exists, type KB, and press *Tab*. The full filename is populated inside Command Prompt and you can press the *Enter* key to launch it.

How it works...

Keyboard shortcuts can greatly increase productivity once you are fluent with them. This is not an extensive list by any means, there are many more key combinations that you can use to launch apps, minimize and maximize windows, and do all sorts of other functions. This is a list to get you started with the most common ones that I employ often. Start using these with your daily tasks and I bet your mouse will start to feel lonely.

If you are interested in exploring more of the Windows Server 2016 key combinations available, this website is a great place to start: `http://technet.microsoft.com/en-us/library/hh831491.aspx`.

Setting your PowerShell Execution Policy

To say that the Windows operating system can be manipulated by PowerShell is a gross understatement. They are fully intertwined, and PowerShell can be useful for so many tasks on your servers. However, the ability to run PowerShell scripts is disabled by default on many machines. The first stumbling block that many new PowerShell administrators bump into is the Execution Policy. It's quite simple: in order to allow PowerShell scripts to run on your server, the Execution Policy must be adjusted to allow that to happen. Let's introduce our first task in PowerShell by using some commands in this recipe that will set this policy for us.

This is also a good introduction to the idea of the verb-noun syntax that PowerShell utilizes. For example, we are going to make use of cmdlets called `Get-ExecutionPolicy` and `Set-ExecutionPolicy`. The `Get-(parameter name)` and `Set-(parameter name)` cmdlets are very common across all facets of cmdlets available in PowerShell. Wrap your mind around this verb-noun syntax and you will be well on your way to figuring out PowerShell on your machines.

Getting ready

We will be working within a PowerShell prompt on our Windows Server 2016 box.

How to do it...

Follow these steps to set the PowerShell Execution Policy:

1. Right-click on the PowerShell icon and choose **Run as administrator**:

2. Type Get-ExecutionPolicy and press *Enter* in order to see the current setting of the PowerShell Execution Policy:

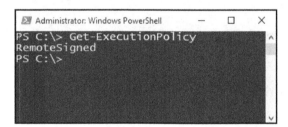

3. You can see that the current Execution Policy is set to **RemoteSigned**. Here is a short description of the different options for the policy:
   - **Remote Signed**: This is the default setting in Server 2016, which allows PowerShell scripts that are locally created to run. If you try running remote scripts, they must be signed by a trusted publisher in order to execute successfully.
   - **All Signed**: With this setting, all scripts will only be allowed to run if they are signed by a trusted publisher.

- **Restricted**: With this setting, PowerShell is locked down so that scripts will not run.
- **Unrestricted**: This setting will allow PowerShell to run scripts, with or without signing.

2. For the purposes of our recipe and to make sure scripts will run for us as we progress through these recipes, let's set our Execution Policy to unrestricted. Go ahead and use this command:

```
Set-ExecutionPolicy Unrestricted
```

The output for this command will be as shown in the below screenshot:

```
Administrator: Windows PowerShell                            —    □    ×
PS C:\> Set-ExecutionPolicy Unrestricted

Execution Policy Change
The execution policy helps protect you from scripts that you do
 not trust. Changing the execution policy might expose you to
the security risks described in the about_Execution_Policies
help topic at http://go.microsoft.com/fwlink/?LinkID=135170. Do
 you want to change the execution policy?
[Y] Yes  [A] Yes to All  [N] No  [L] No to All  [S] Suspend
[?] Help(default is "N"): y
PS C:\>
```

How it works...

The PowerShell Execution Policy is a simple setting and easy to change, but can make a world of difference when it comes to running your first scripts. If configured to be more restrictive than you intend, you will have trouble getting your scripts to run and may think that you have mistyped something, when in fact the issue is only the policy. On the other hand, in an effort to make your servers as secure as possible, on machines where you don't need to execute PowerShell scripts, it makes sense to restrict this access. You may also want to read some additional information on the signing of scripts to see whether creating and executing signed scripts would make more sense in your own environment. There are some in-built server functions that rely on a certain level of security with your Execution Policy. Setting your policy to unrestricted on all of your servers could result in some functions not working properly, and you may have to increase that level of security back to remote signed.

Building and executing your first PowerShell script

Command Prompt and PowerShell are both great command-line interfaces that can acquire and configure information about our servers. Most of us are familiar with creating some simple batch files that are driven by **Command Prompt**, essentially programming out small tasks within these batch files to automate a series of commands. This saves time later as we do not have to type out the commands line by line, especially for common tasks or for items that we need to run during login.

PowerShell has similar functionality, the ability to write out multiple lines of PowerShell cmdlets inside a script file. We can then launch this script file as we would a batch file, automating tasks while taking advantage of the additional features that PowerShell brings to the table over **Command Prompt**. These PowerShell scripts are put together inside .ps1 files; let's build a simple one together to get a feel for running these scripts.

Getting ready

Our work with PowerShell today will be accomplished from a Windows Server 2016 machine. PowerShell is installed by default with Windows, and there is nothing further that we need to install.

How to do it...

Follow these steps to build and execute our first PowerShell script:

1. Open the Start menu and type `Windows PowerShell ISE`. Right-click to launch this tool as an administrator. **Windows PowerShell ISE** is an editor for PowerShell scripts that is much more useful than opening a simple text editor such as Notepad in order to build our script:

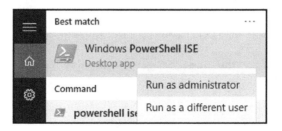

2. Navigate to **File** | **New** from the menus in order to open a blank .ps1 script file.

3. In your first line, type the following: Write-Host "Hello! Here is the current date and time:".

4. From the toolbar menu, click the green arrow that says **Run Script**. Alternatively, you can simply press the *F5* button. When you run the script, the command and output are displayed in the lower portion of the ISE window:

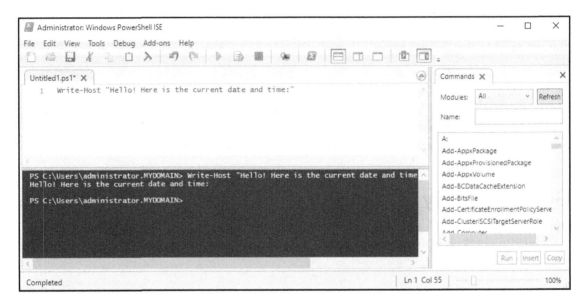

Cool! Okay, so far it's actually pretty lame. It's just reflecting the text that we told it to echo, but it worked. That is the nice thing about using the ISE editing tool rather than a generic text editor, you have the ability to quickly test run scripts as you make modifications.

5. Now let's add some additional lines into our script to give us the information we are looking for. You can see a list of available commands on the right side of the screen if you would like to browse through what is available, but for our example simply change your script to include the following:

```
Write-Host "Hello! Here is the current date and time:"
Get-Date
Write-Host "The name of your computer is:"
hostname
```

6. Press the **Run Script** button again to see the new output:

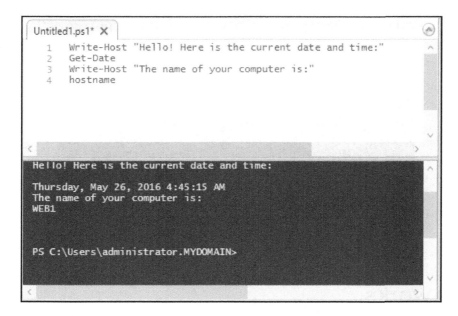

7. Now navigate to **File | Save** and save your new .ps1 PowerShell script out to the Desktop.
8. Let's test this script by launching it from within a real PowerShell command window. Right-click on your PowerShell icon in the Taskbar and choose **Run as administrator**.
9. Browse to the location of the script file, I placed mine on the Desktop. Then launch the script by inputting .filename. In my case, it looks like this: .time.ps1.

Remember that the *Tab* key can be our friend in this. When browsing to your Desktop, all you need to do is input the first letter of your script filename, and then press *Tab*. Since I named my script `Time.ps1`, all I had to do was press the *T* and then press *Tab*, then *Enter*.

```
Administrator: Windows PowerShell                          —    □    ×
PS C:\users\administrator.MYDOMAIN\Desktop> .\Time.ps1
Hello! Here is the current date and time:

Thursday, May 26, 2016 4:49:46 AM
The name of your computer is:
WEB1


PS C:\users\administrator.MYDOMAIN\Desktop> _
```

How it works...

In this recipe, we created a very simple PowerShell script and saved it on our server for execution. While in practice getting time and date information from your server may come faster by using the standalone `Get-Date` cmdlet, we use this recipe to give a small taste of the ISE and to get your scripting juices flowing. Expanding upon the ideas presented here will start to save you valuable time and keystrokes as you identify more and more ways to automate the tasks and information gathering that are part of your daily routines. The possibilities of PowerShell are practically limitless, so make sure that you open it up and start becoming familiar with the interfaces and tools associated with it right away!

Searching for PowerShell cmdlets with Get-Help

With this recipe, let's take a minute to use `Get-Help` inside PowerShell in order to, well, get some help! I see both new and experienced PowerShell administrators going to the Web a lot in order to find commands and the parameters of those commands. The Internet is great, and there is a ton of data out there about how to use PowerShell, but in many cases the information that you are looking for resides right inside PowerShell itself. By using the `Get-Help` cmdlet combined with the functions you are running or searching for, you might not have to open that web browser after all.

Getting ready

We will be running some commands from inside PowerShell on a Windows Server 2016 machine.

How to do it...

To use the Get-Help function inside PowerShell, run the following steps:

1. Launch a PowerShell prompt.
2. Type Get-Help.
3. You're finished! No, I'm just kidding. Using Get-Help by itself will present you with some helpful data about the Get-Help command, but that's not really what we are looking for, is it? How about using Get-Help with a search parameter, like this:

    Get-Help Computer

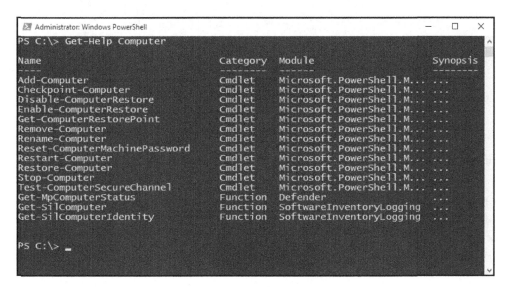

Cool! That searched the available cmdlets and presented us with a list of the ones that contain the word Computer. Nice!

4. Now, what if we wanted to find out some more particular information about one of these cmdlets? Maybe about `Restart-Computer`; that sounds like something we might use often. Use the following command:

```
Get-Help Restart-Computer
```

```
Administrator: Windows PowerShell                           —    □    ×
PS C:\> Get-Help Restart-Computer

NAME
      Restart-Computer

SYNTAX
      Restart-Computer [[-ComputerName] <string[]>] [[-Credential]
      <pscredential>] [-DcomAuthentication {Default | None | Connect | Call |
      Packet | PacketIntegrity | PacketPrivacy | Unchanged}] [-Impersonation
      {Default | Anonymous | Identify | Impersonate | Delegate}]
      [-WsmanAuthentication {Default | Basic | Negotiate | CredSSP | Digest |
      Kerberos}] [-Protocol {DCOM | WSMan}] [-Force] [-Wait] [-Timeout <int>]
      [-For {Wmi | WinRM | PowerShell}] [-Delay <int16>] [-WhatIf] [-Confirm]
      [<CommonParameters>]

      Restart-Computer [[-ComputerName] <string[]>] [[-Credential]
      <pscredential>] [-AsJob] [-DcomAuthentication {Default | None | Connect |
      Call | Packet | PacketIntegrity | PacketPrivacy | Unchanged}]
      Delegate}] [-Force] [-ThrottleLimit <int>] [-WhatIf] [-Confirm]
      [<CommonParameters>]
```

Now we're really cooking! This is wonderful information. Basically, this is exactly what you would find if you were looking for information about the `Restart-Computer` cmdlet and went searching on TechNet for it.

How it works...

The `Get-Help` cmdlet in PowerShell can be used with virtually any command in order to find out more information about that particular function. I often use it when the specific name of a cmdlet that I want to use escapes my memory. By using `Get-Help` as a search function, it will present a list of available cmdlets that include the keyword you specified. This is a brilliant addition to PowerShell, and makes it so much more powerful than Command Prompt.

Also included with the `Get-Help` files are all of the special syntax and parameter options for each cmdlet that you might be working with. This saves you having to go to the web in order to search for these functions, and it is just way more fun doing it at the command line than in a web browser.

2
Core Infrastructure Tasks

Windows Server 2016 has many roles and features that can be used to accomplish all sorts of different tasks in your network. This chapter reflects on the most common infrastructure tasks needed to create a successful Windows Active Directory environment by using Server 2016. In this chapter, we will cover the following recipes:

- Configuring a combination Domain Controller, DNS server, and DHCP server
- Adding a second Domain Controller
- Organizing your computers with Organizational Units
- Creating an A or AAAA record in DNS
- Creating and using a CNAME record in DNS
- Creating a DHCP scope to assign addresses to computers
- Creating a DHCP reservation for a specific server or resource
- Pre-staging a computer account in Active Directory
- Using PowerShell to create a new Active Directory user
- Using PowerShell to view system uptime

Introduction

There are a number of technologies in Windows Server 2016 that you *need to know* if you plan to ever work in a Windows environment. These are technologies such as **Active Directory Domain Services (AD DS)**, **Domain Name System (DNS)**, and **Dynamic Host Configuration Protocol (DHCP)**. If you haven't noticed already, everything in the Windows world has an acronym. In fact, you may only recognize these items by their acronyms, and that's okay.

Nobody calls DHCP the Dynamic Host Configuration Protocol anyway. But do you know how to build these services and bring a Windows Server infrastructure online from scratch, with only a piece of hardware and a Windows Server 2016 installation disk to guide your way? This is why we are here today. I would like to instruct you on taking your first server and turning it into everything that you need to run a Microsoft network.

Every company and network is different and has different requirements. Some will get by with a single server to host a myriad of roles, while others have thousands of servers at their disposal and will have every role split up into clusters of servers, each of which has a single purpose in life. Whatever your situation, this will get us back to the basics on setting up the core infrastructure technologies that are needed in any Microsoft-centric network.

Configuring a combination Domain Controller, DNS server, and DHCP server

The directory structure that Microsoft networks use to house their users and computer accounts is called **Active Directory (AD)**, and the directory information is controlled and managed by **Domain Controller (DC)** servers. Two other server roles that almost always go hand-in-hand with Active Directory are DNS and DHCP, and in many networks, these three roles are combined on each server where they reside. A lot of small businesses have always made do with a single server containing all three of these roles, but in recent years, virtualization has become so easy that almost everyone runs at least two DCs, for redundancy purposes. And if you are going to have two DCs, you may as well put the DNS and DHCP roles on them both to make those services redundant as well. But I'm getting ahead of myself. For this recipe, let's get started with building these services by installing the roles and configuring them for the first time: the first DC/DNS/DHCP server in our network.

Getting ready

The only prerequisite here is an online Windows Server 2016 that we can use. We want it to be plugged into a network and have a static IP address assigned so that as you add new computers to this network, they have a way of communicating with the domain we are about to create. Also, make sure to set the hostname of the server now. Once you create a domain on this controller, you will not be able to change the name at a later date.

How to do it...

Let's configure our first DC/DNS/DHCP server by performing the following set of instructions:

1. Add the roles all at once. To do this, open up **Server Manager** and click on your link to add some new roles to this server. Now check all three: **Active Directory Domain Services**, **DHCP Server**, and **DNS Server**:

2. When you click on **Active Directory Domain Services**, you will be prompted whether you want to install some supporting items. Go ahead and click on the **Add Features** button to allow this:

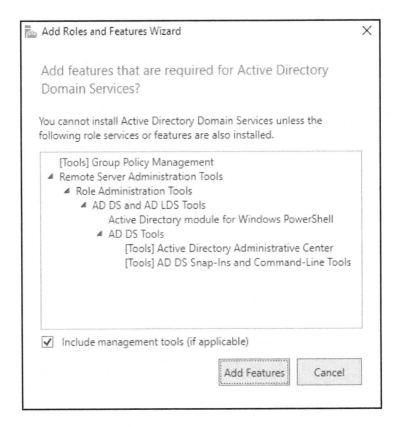

3. You are going to click **Next** through the following few screens. We don't have to add any additional features, so you can read and click through the informational screens that tell you about these new roles.

4. Once satisfied with the installation summary, press the **Install** button on the last page of the wizard.

5. Following installation, your progress summary screen shows a window with a
   couple of links on it. They are **Promote this server to a domain controller** and
   Complete DHCP configuration. We are going to click on the first link to promote
   this machine to be a DC:

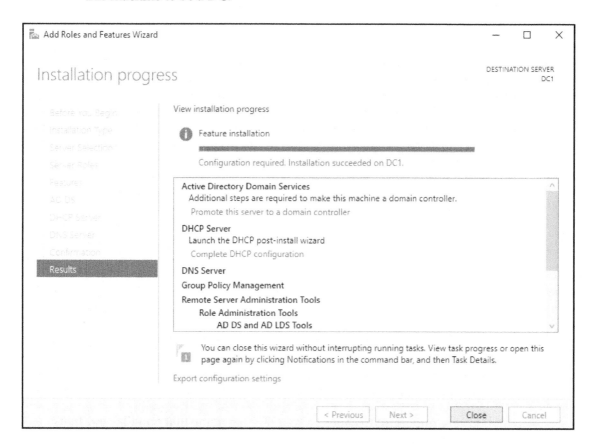

6. Now we are taken into the configuration of our DC. Since this is the very first DC in our entire network, we choose the option **Add a new forest**. At this point, we also have to specify a name for our root domain:

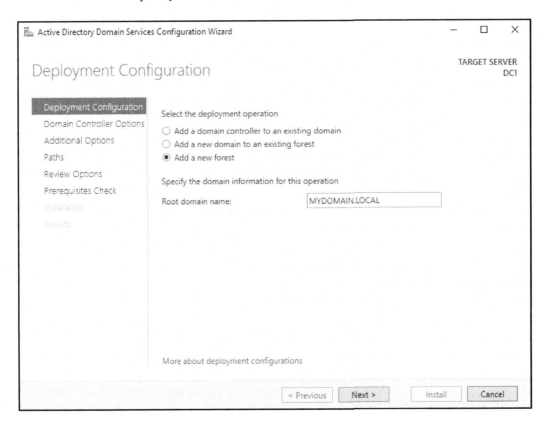

It is very important to choose a root domain name that you like and that makes sense for your installation. Whatever you enter here will more than likely be your domain name forever and always!!

7. This might be a good opportunity for a little side-bar of definitions and explanations. You can think of a *forest* as the top level of your Active Directory structure. Within that forest, you are setting up a *domain*, which is the container within your forest that contains your user, computer, and other accounts that will be joined to the domain. You can contain multiple domains within a forest, and multiple forests can share information and talk to each other by using something called a trust.

8. You can see that I have named my domain MYDOMAIN.LOCAL. The .local is important to discuss for a minute. It is really just a common specification that many companies use to clarify that this domain is an internal network, not a public one. However, I could have just as easily named it CONTOSO.COM, or JORDAN.PRIV, or many different things.

9. Another practice that I see often is for companies to use the same domain name inside their network as they do publicly. So basically, whatever their website ends in, that is their public domain name. You could certainly set up the internal domain name to be the same. This practice is commonly referred to as *split-brain DNS*. It used to be something that Microsoft warned against doing, but many companies do it this way, and all of the technology has evolved around this so that the Microsoft networking parts and pieces will all work just fine with split-brain DNS these days, though it does usually take additional consideration when setting up any new piece of technology.

One last important note: it is **not** recommended to set up your domain as a single label name, for example, if I had called it just MYDOMAIN. While this is technically possible, it presents many problems down the road and is not recommended by Microsoft.

10. On the **Domain Controller Options** screen, you can choose to lower the functional level of your forest or domain, but this is not recommended unless you have a specific reason to do so. You must also specify a DSRM password on this screen in case it is ever needed for recovery. You will receive a **DNS Options** warning message on the next page. This is normal because we are turning on the first DC and DNS server in our environment.

11. The following two screens for **NetBIOS** and **Paths** can be left as the default unless you have a reason to change their settings.

12. Once you have reviewed the installation plan, go for it! There may be some informational and warning messages that show themselves, but you should see a green check mark telling you **All prerequisite checks passed successfully**, which means you are ready to proceed. When the server is finished being promoted to a DC, it will have to restart.

13. Following the restart, you will have noticed that you are now forced to log in to the server as a domain account. Once a server has been promoted to a DC, it no longer contains local user accounts on the system. All logins to the server from this point forward will have to be user accounts within the domain. Go ahead and log in as such.

14. Inside **Server Manager,** you will have a notification up top to **Complete DHCP configuration**. Go ahead and click on that:

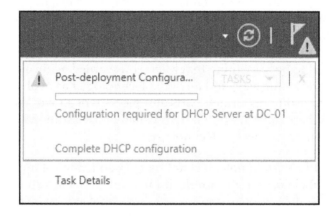

15. You don't have to specify anything in this wizard. Simply click through the steps.

How it works...

Configuring your first DC is essential to having a successful Microsoft Windows network. Now that the roles are installed for AD, DNS, and DHCP, we have the core infrastructure in place to start joining computers to the domain, adding users to the network, and shuttling around some network traffic! Each of these technologies has enough depth to warrant their own book, so there is no way that we can cover everything here. I hope that this tutorial will get you comfortable with enabling these system-critical functions in your own network. Having the ability to create a network from scratch is priceless ammunition to a server administrator.

See also

It is also possible to install Active Directory on your DCs through the use of PowerShell. Since we are discussing the use of PowerShell throughout this book to start utilizing it for some day-to-day tasks, make sure to check out the following links and try doing it this way on the next DC that you want to create:

- http://technet.microsoft.com/en-us/library/hh974719.aspx
- http://technet.microsoft.com/en-us/library/hh472162.aspx#BKMK_PS

Adding a second Domain Controller

AD is the core of your network. It has ties to everything! As such, it makes sense that you would want this to be as redundant as possible. In Windows Server 2016, creating a secondary DC is so easy that you really have no reason not to do it. Can you imagine rebuilding your directory following a single server hardware failure where you have 100 user accounts and computers that are all part of the domain that just failed? How about with 1,000 or even 10,000 users? That could take weeks to clean up, and you'll probably never get it back exactly the way it was before. Additionally, while you are stuck in the middle of this downtime, you will have all kinds of trouble inside your network since your user and computer accounts are relying on AD, which would then be offline. Here are the steps to take a second server in your network and join it to the existing domain that is running on the primary DC to create our redundant, secondary DC. The larger your network gets, the more domain controller servers you are going to have.

Getting ready

Two Server 2016 machines are needed for this. The first we will assume is running Active Directory and DNS already, like the one we set up in our previous recipe. The second server is online, plugged into the same network, and has been named DC2.

How to do it...

To create a redundant secondary DC, perform the following steps:

1. Open **Server Manager** on DC02 and click the link to **Add roles and features**.

2. Click **Next** a few times until you get to the screen where we are selecting the role that we want to install. Let's choose both **Active Directory Domain Services** and **DNS Server**. It is very common for each DC to also run DNS so that you have redundancy for both services. Both of these roles will prompt for additional features, so make sure you press the **Add Features** button when it prompts you to allow the installation of those extra components:

3. We do not require any other features, so click **Next** through the remaining screens and then click on **Install** on the last page.

4. Once the installation is finished, you have a link to click on that says **Promote this server to a domain controller**. Go ahead and click on that link:

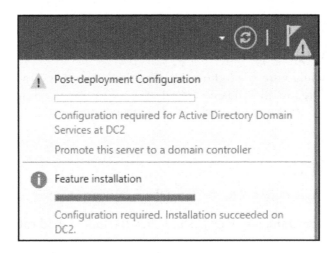

5. For this second DC, we are going to choose the **Add a domain controller to an existing domain** option. Then in the **Domain** field, specify the name of the domain that is running on your primary DC. You must also specify a domain user account in the credentials field to validate against the domain:

Select the deployment operation

◉ Add a domain controller to an existing domain
◯ Add a new domain to an existing forest
◯ Add a new forest

Specify the domain information for this operation

Domain: MYDOMAIN.LOCAL | Select... |

If you receive an error message that a DC for the domain could not be contacted, you probably haven't specified a DNS address in your TCP/IP settings. Add your primary DC's IP address in as your primary DNS server and it should work.

6. The rest of the steps reflect the same options we chose when creating our first DC in the previous recipe. Once you are finished stepping through the wizard, you will have a secondary DC and DNS server online and running.

How it works...

Creating redundancy for Active Directory is critical to the success of your network. Hardware fails, we all know it. A good practice for any company is to run two DCs so that everyone continues to work in the event of a server failure. An even better practice is to take this a step further and create more DCs, some of them in different sites perhaps, and maybe even make use of some **Read-Only Domain Controllers (RODC)** in your smaller, less secure sites. See the following link for some additional information on using an RODC in your environment: `http://technet.microsoft.com/en-us/library/cc754719(v=ws.10).aspx`.

Organizing your computers with Organizational Units

AD is the structure in which all of your user, computer, and server accounts reside. As you add new users and computers into your domain, they will be automatically placed into generic storage containers. You could get away with leaving all of your objects in their default locations, but there are a lot of advantages to putting a little time and effort into creating an organizational structure.

In this recipe, we will create some **Organizational Units (OUs)** inside Active Directory and move our existing objects into these OUs so that we can create some structure.

Getting ready

We will need a DC online for this recipe, which is a Server 2016 machine with the Active Directory Domain Services role installed. Specifically, I will be using the DC1 server that we prepped in the earlier *Configuring a combination Domain Controller, DNS server, and DHCP server* recipe.

How to do it...

Let's get comfortable working with OUs by creating some of our own, as follows:

1. Open **Active Directory Users and Computers**. This can be launched from the **Tools** menu inside **Server Manager**. As you can see, there are some pre-defined containers and OUs in here:

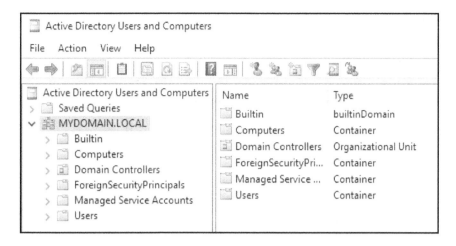

Alternatively, you can also open **Active Directory Users and Computers** by running `dsa.msc` from a command prompt or the Start screen.

2. We can already see that the DC servers have been segmented off into their own OU. If we look in our `Computers` folder, however, we can see that currently, all of the other systems we have joined to the domain have been lumped together:

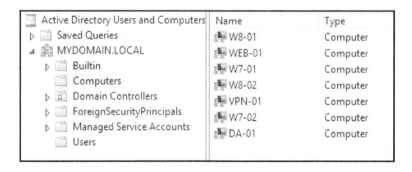

3. Currently, it's hard to tell which machine accomplishes what purpose. A better naming scheme might help, but what if you are working in an environment where there are hundreds of objects already? We want to break these machines up into appropriate groups so that we have better management over them in the future. Right-click on the name of your domain in the left-hand window pane, then navigate to **New | Organizational Unit**.

4. Input a name for your new OU and click **OK**. I am going to create a few new OUs called `Windows 7 Desktops`, `Windows 7 Laptops`, `Windows 8 Desktops`, `Windows 8 Laptops`, `Windows 10 Desktops`, `Windows 10 Laptops`, `Web Servers`, and `Remote Access Servers`:

5. Now for each object that you want to move, simply find it, right-click on it, and then click on **Move...**:

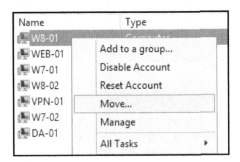

6. Choose which OU you would like this object to move into and click **OK**.

How it works...

The actual work involved with creating OUs and moving objects around between them isn't complicated at all. What is much more important about this recipe is prompting you to think about which way works best for you to set up these OUs to make the best organizational sense for your environment. By breaking our computer accounts out into pinpointed groups, we are able, in the future, to easily do things such as discover how many web servers we have running, or do some quick reporting on how many user accounts we have in the sales group. We could even apply different Group Policy settings to different computer sets based on what OU they are contained within. Both reporting and applying settings can be greatly improved upon by making good use of Organizational Units inside AD.

Creating an A or AAAA record in DNS

Most folks working in IT are familiar with using the `ping` command to test network connectivity. If you are trying to test the connection between your computer and another, you can ping it from a Command Prompt and test whether or not it replies. This assumes that the firewalls in your computers and network allow the ping to respond correctly, which generally is true. If you are inside a domain network and ping a device by its name, that name resolves to an IP address, which is the device's address on the network. But what tells your computer which IP address corresponds to which name? This is where DNS comes in. Any time your computer makes a request for a name, whether it is you pinging another computer or your Outlook e-mail client requesting the name of your Exchange Server, your computer always reaches out to your network's DNS servers and asks, "How do I get to this name?".

DNS contains a list of records that tell the computers in your network what IP addresses correspond to what names. By far the most common type of DNS record is called a **Host** record. When the Host record resolves to an IPv4 address, such as `192.168.0.1`, it is called an **A record**. When the Host record resolves to an IPv6 address, such as `2003:836b:2:8100::2`, it is called an **AAAA record**. This is usually pronounced *quad A*.

Understanding how to create and troubleshoot Host records in DNS is something that every Windows server administrator needs to know. Let's take a minute to create and test one of these DNS records so that we can experience firsthand how this all works together.

Getting ready

We have a DC online, which also has the DNS role installed. This is all we need to create the DNS record, but we will also make use of a Windows 10 client computer and a web server to do the name resolution testing.

How to do it...

To create and test a DNS record, perform these steps:

1. There is a new web server plugged into the network, but it is not yet joined to the domain and so it has not been registered to DNS. The name of this web server is Web1. Open up Command Prompt and type ping web1. As expected, because there is no Host record in DNS for this server yet, our ping request does not resolve to anything:

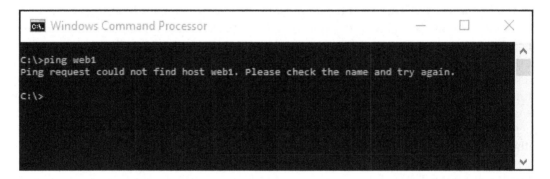

2. Now head to the DNS server and open up the **DNS** console from the **Tools** menu.
3. Inside **Forward Lookup Zones**, you should see your domain listed. Double-click on the name of your domain to see your existing DNS records:

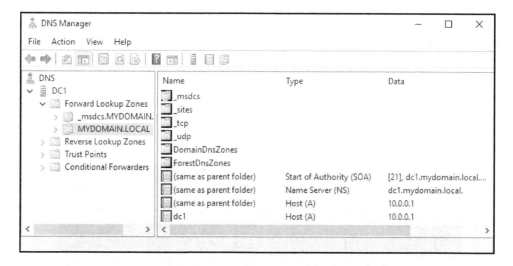

4. Right-click on your domain, then click on **New Host (A or AAAA)...**
5. Input the server name into the top field and the IP address where it is running into the bottom field. Then click **Add Host**:

If you are running IPv6 on your network and want to create a AAAA record instead, you use this exact same process. Simply enter the IPv6 address into the IP address field, instead of the IPv4 address.

6. Now that our new Host record has been created, let's test it out! Going back to our client computer, type `ping web1` again. You will see your output as shown in the following screenshot:

```
C:\>ping web1

Pinging web1.MYDOMAIN.LOCAL [10.0.0.5] with 32 bytes of data:
Reply from 10.0.0.5: bytes=32 time<1ms TTL=128
Reply from 10.0.0.5: bytes=32 time<1ms TTL=128
Reply from 10.0.0.5: bytes=32 time<1ms TTL=128
Reply from 10.0.0.5: bytes=32 time<1ms TTL=128

Ping statistics for 10.0.0.5:
    Packets: Sent = 4, Received = 4, Lost = 0 (0% loss),
Approximate round trip times in milli-seconds:
    Minimum = 0ms, Maximum = 0ms, Average = 0ms

C:\>
```

How it works...

Any time a computer in a domain network requests to communicate with a hostname, DNS is the party responsible for pointing it in the right direction. If you or your applications are having trouble contacting the servers they need, this is one of the first places you will want to look into. Understanding DNS Host records is something that will be necessary when working with any networking technology. If you are working within an Active Directory integrated DNS zone, which most of you will be, then any time you add a computer or server to the domain, their name will be automatically plugged into DNS for you. In these cases, you will not have to manually create them, but it is still important to understand how that works, in case you need to troubleshoot them later.

In this recipe, we have only talked about the most common form of DNS record, but there are others you may want to learn and test as well. In fact, take a look at our next recipe for information on another useful type of DNS record, the CNAME.

There are a couple of other name resolution functions in the Windows operating system that may cause resolution to happen before a hostname request gets to the DNS server. For example, if someone has created a static name and IP record inside a client computer's host file, it will resolve to the specified IP address, no matter what is in the DNS server. This is because the host file has priority over DNS. Also, there is a special table called the **Name Resolution Policy Table** (**NRPT**) that is used by DirectAccess client computers, and it works in a similar way. Name resolution requests pass through the host file and through the NRPT before making their way to DNS. If one of the former tables has an entry for the name that is being requested, they will resolve it before the computer sends the request to the DNS server for resolution. So if you are troubleshooting a name that doesn't resolve properly, keep those additional items in mind when looking for the answer to your problem.

See also

- The *Creating and using a CNAME record in DNS* recipe

Creating and using a CNAME record in DNS

Now that we are familiar with moving around a little bit inside the DNS management tool, we are going to create and test another type of record. This one is called a **CNAME**, and it is easiest to think of this one as an alias record. Rather than taking a DNS name and pointing it at an IP address, as we do with a host record, with a CNAME, we are going to take a DNS name and point it at another DNS name! Why would this be necessary? If you are hosting multiple services on a single server but want those services to be contacted by using different names, CNAME records can be your best friend.

Getting ready

We are going to make use of the same environment that we used to create our *A* records in the *Creating an A or AAAA record in DNS* recipe. There is a DC/DNS server online where we are going to create our records. Also running is WEB1, a server where we are hosting a website as well as some file shares. We will also use a Windows 10 client to test out our CNAME records after they have been created.

How to do it...

To create and test a CNAME record, perform the following instructions:

1. WEB1 is hosting a website and a file share. Currently, the only DNS record that exists for WEB1 is the primary *A* record, so users have to type in the WEB1 name to access both the website and the file shares. Our goal is to create aliases for these services by using CNAME records in DNS. First, we log into the DNS server and launch **DNS Manager**.

2. Once inside **DNS Manager**, expand **Forward Lookup Zones** and then your domain name so that we can see the list of DNS records that exist already.

3. Now right-click on your domain and select **New Alias (CNAME)...**

4. We would like our users to be able to browse the website by typing in `http://intranet`. So in our CNAME record, we want the **Alias name** to be `INTRANET` and the **FQDN for target host** to be `WEB1.MYDOMAIN.LOCAL`, which is the server where the website is being hosted:

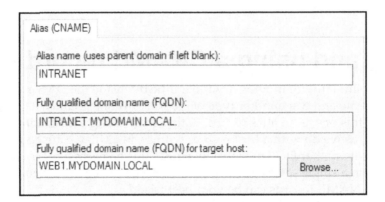

5. We also want our file shares to be accessible by using `\FILESERVERSHARE`, so that the actual name of the server hosting this share is not visible to the users. Create another CNAME record with the **Alias name** field as `FILESERVER`, and the **FQDN for target host** field as `WEB1.MYDOMAIN.LOCAL`.

6. Log into the test client machine and give it a try. Users are now able to open up Internet Explorer and successfully browse to `http://intranet`. They are also able to open File Explorer and access `\fileservershare`.

How it works...

We have a server in our environment called **WEB1**. There is a website running on this server. It is also hosting a file share called **SHARE**. By creating a couple of quick CNAME records inside DNS, we are able to give users the ability to use some intuitive names to access these resources. By following the preceding instructions, we have masked the actual server name from the users, making knowledge of that name unnecessary. Masking internal hostnames of servers is also considered a security best practice in many organizations.

See also

- The *Creating an A or AAAA record in DNS* recipe

Creating a DHCP scope to assign addresses to computers

In the *Configuring a combination Domain Controller, DNS server, and DHCP server* recipes, we installed the DHCP role onto a server called DC1. Without some configuration, however, that role isn't doing anything. In most companies that I work with, all of the servers have statically assigned IP addresses, which are IPs entered by hand into the NIC properties. This way, those servers always retain the same IP address. But what about client machines that might move around, or even move in and out of the network? DHCP is a mechanism that the clients can reach out to in order to obtain IP addressing information for the network that they are currently plugged into.

This way, users or admins don't have to worry about configuring IP settings on the client machine, as they are configured automatically by the DHCP server. In order for our DHCP server to hand out IP addresses, we need to configure a scope.

Getting ready

We have a Server 2016 machine online with the DHCP role installed. We will also be testing using a Windows 10 client machine to ensure that it is able to acquire IP address information properly from the server.

How to do it...

Perform the following steps to create and configure a DHCP scope to assign addresses to client computers:

1. Drop down the **Tools** menu inside Server Manager, then click on **DHCP**. This opens the DHCP management console.

2. Expand the left-hand pane, where the name of your DHCP server is listed. You will see sections for **IPv4** and **IPv6**. For our network, we are sticking with IPv4, so we right-click on that and choose the option for **New Scope...**:

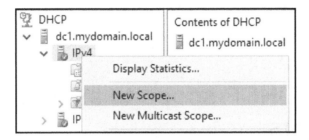

3. Start the **New Scope Wizard** screen by creating a name for your scope. This can be anything you like.

4. Enter a range of IP addresses that you would like the DHCP server to hand out to computers. The **Subnet mask** field will likely populate automatically; just double-check to make sure it is accurate:

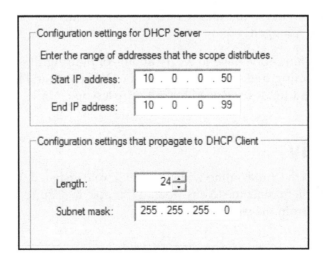

5. On the **Add Exclusions and Delay** screen, if there are any IP addresses within the scope you just defined that you do not want handed out, specify them here. For example, if you are going to use .50 through .99, but you already have a print server running on .75, you could exclude .75 on this screen so that DHCP doesn't try to hand out the .75 address to a client computer.

6. Now set a time in your **Lease Duration** field. This is the amount of time in between DHCP *refreshes* for a client computer. If a particular computer leaves the network and comes back within its lease duration, it will be given the same IP address that it had last time. If you're not sure about this one, leave it set at the default and you can adjust it later.

7. Next, we will populate the rest of the IP information that the client computers need to receive on our network. Fill out fields for **Router (Default Gateway), Domain Name and DNS Servers,** and **WINS Servers,** if necessary.

8. The last item to choose is **Yes, I want to activate this scope now**. We're in business!

9. As a quick test, let's boot a client computer onto this network whose NIC has not been configured with a static IP. If we take a look at its IP configuration, we can see that it has successfully received IP addressing information from our DHCP server automatically:

```
Ethernet adapter Ethernet:

   Connection-specific DNS Suffix  . : MYDOMAIN.LOCAL
   Link-local IPv6 Address . . . . . : fe80::5465:727f:ba9:a073%4
   IPv4 Address. . . . . . . . . . . : 10.0.0.50
   Subnet Mask . . . . . . . . . . . : 255.255.255.0
   Default Gateway . . . . . . . . . : 10.0.0.254
```

How it works...

DHCP is one of the core infrastructure roles that almost everyone uses inside their networks. While we have only scratched the surface here of what DHCP is capable of, the ability to automatically hand out IP addresses to connecting client computers is DHCP's core functionality. Installing the role and creating a scope are our primary steps to make use of DHCP. Take a look at our next recipe for one of the advanced functions that can be accomplished within your scope.

Creating a DHCP reservation for a specific server or resource

In a simple DHCP scope, any device that connects and asks for an IP address is handed whatever IP is next available within the scope. If you have a device for which you always want to keep the same IP address, you could manually configure the NIC properties with a static IP address. Otherwise, a more centralized way to assign a particular IP to the same device on a long-term basis is to use a **DHCP reservation**. Using a reservation in DHCP to assign an IP to a device makes a lot of sense, because you can see that reservation right in the DHCP console and you don't have to worry about keeping track of the static IP addresses that you have configured out in the field. Let's walk through configuring a quick reservation so that you are familiar with this process.

Getting ready

We will be using a Windows Server 2016 machine as our DHCP server where we will create the DHCP reservation. Additionally, we will use our WEB1 server to be the recipient of this reservation by assigning WEB1 to IP address 10.0.0.85.

How to do it...

To create a DHCP reservation for a specific server or resource, perform these instructions:

1. Open the **DHCP** manager tool.
2. Expand the left-hand pane down into the DHCP scope that we created earlier. Under this scope, you will see a folder called Reservations. Right-click on Reservations and click on **New Reservation...**
3. Populate the fields. Your **Reservation name** field can contain anything descriptive. Fill out the **IP address** field with the IP address you want to reserve for this purpose. The last important piece of information is the **MAC address** field. This must be the MAC address of the device for which you want to receive this particular IP address. Since WEB1 is a Windows Server 2016 machine, we can get our MAC address by doing ipconfig /all on WEB1:

```
Ethernet adapter Ethernet:

   Connection-specific DNS Suffix  . :
   Description . . . . . . . . . . . : Microsoft Hyper-V Network Adapter
   Physical Address. . . . . . . . . : 00-15-5D-AC-20-01
```

4. You can see **Physical Address.........: 00-15-5D-AC-20-01** in Command Prompt—this is our MAC address for WEB1. Use it to finish populating the DHCP reservation.

5. Click on **Add** and you will see your new reservation listed in the **DHCP** management console.

6. Now make sure that the NIC on WEB1 is set to **Obtain an IP address automatically**. When WEB1 reaches out to DHCP to grab an IP address, it will now always receive 10.0.0.85 because of the reservation, rather than getting whatever IP address is next available within the DHCP scope.

How it works...

Typically, whenever a client computer is set to obtain an IP address automatically, it reaches out and looks for a DHCP server that hands to the client whatever IP address is free and next in the list. This causes DHCP clients to change their IP addresses on a regular basis. For desktop computers, this is usually fine. In many cases, however, it is beneficial to reserve particular IP addresses for specific devices, thereby ensuring they always receive the same IP address. Creating DHCP reservations is a good practice for servers, and also for many static devices on the network, such as print server boxes and telephony equipment.

Pre-staging a computer account in Active Directory

Joining computers to your domain is going to be a very normal task for any IT professional, enough that all of you are probably familiar with the process of doing so. What you may not realize, though, is that when you join computers or servers to your domain, they get lumped automatically into a generic Computers container inside AD. Sometimes this doesn't present any problem at all and all of your machines can reside inside this Computers container folder forever. Most of the time, however, organizations will set up policies that filter down into the Computers container automatically. When this is the case, these policies and settings will immediately apply to all computers that you join to your domain. For a desktop computer, this might be desired behavior. When configuring a new server, though, this can present big problems.

Let's say you are interested in turning on a new remote access server that is going to be running DirectAccess. You have a domain policy in place that disables the Windows Firewall on computers that get added to the `Computers` container. In this case, if you turned on your new remote access server and simply joined it to the domain, it would immediately apply the policy to disable Windows Firewall, because it is no different than a regular client computer in your network. DirectAccess requires Windows Firewall to be enabled, and so you have effectively broken your server before you even finish configuring it! You would eventually realize this mistake and move the server into a different OU that doesn't have the firewall squash policy; however, this doesn't necessarily mean that all the changes the policy put into place will be reversed. You may still have trouble with that server on an ongoing basis.

The preceding example is the reason why we are going to follow this recipe. If we pre-stage the computer account for our new remote access server, we can choose where it will reside inside Active Directory even before we join it to the domain. **Pre-staging** is a way of creating the computer's object inside Active Directory before you go to the actual server and click **Join**. When you do this, as soon as the request to join the domain comes in, Active Directory already knows exactly where to place that computer account. This way, you can make sure that the account resides inside an OU that is not going to apply the firewall policy and keep your new server running properly.

Getting ready

We will use a Server 2016 DC to pre-stage the computer account. Following the preceding example, we will use a second server that we are going to join to our domain, which we plan to turn into a remote access server in the future.

How to do it...

To pre-stage a computer account so that it resides inside AD, perform the following steps:

1. Open the **Active Directory Users and Computers** tool on a DC.
2. Choose a location in which you want to place this new server. I am going to use an OU that I created called **RemoteAccessServers**.
3. Right-click on your OU and navigate to **New | Computer**.

4. Enter the name of your new server. Make sure this matches the hostname you are going to assign as you build this new server so that when it joins the domain, it matches up with this entry in AD. Take note on this screen that you also have the ability to determine which user or group has permission to join this new machine to the domain, if you want to set a restriction here:

5. Click **OK**, and that's it! Your object for this new server is entered into AD, waiting for a computer account to join the domain that matches the name.

6. The last step is building the RA1 server and joining it to the domain, just like you would with any computer or server. When you do so, it will utilize this pre-existing account in the **Remote Access Servers** OU, instead of placing a new entry into the generic Computers container.

How it works...

Pre-staging computer accounts in Active Directory is an important function when building new servers. It is sometimes critical to the long-term health of these servers for them to steer clear of the default domain policies and settings that you apply to your regular computer accounts. By taking a quick 30 seconds prior to joining a new server to the domain to pre-stage its account in AD, you ensure the correct placement of the system so that it fits your organizational structure. This will keep the system running properly as you continue to configure it for whatever job you are trying to accomplish.

Using PowerShell to create a new Active Directory user

Creating new user accounts in Active Directory is pretty standard stuff, but doing it the traditional way requires a lot of mouse clicks. Since we know that PowerShell can be used to accomplish anything within Windows Server 2016, but not many people actually employ it regularly, let's use this common task as a recipe to be accomplished with PowerShell rather than the GUI.

Getting ready

We will use PowerShell on our Windows Server 2016 DC in order to create this new user account.

How to do it...

Follow along to create a new user account in Active Directory by using the PowerShell command prompt:

1. Launch a PowerShell command prompt as an Administrator.
2. Enter the following command in order to create a new user account with very simple parameters:

```
New-ADUser -Name "John Smith" -UserPrincipalName
    "jsmith@mydomain.local" -SamAccountName "jsmith"
```

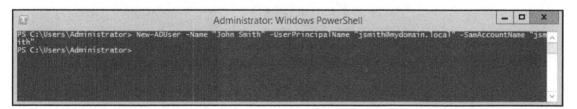

3. If you open up the GUI for **Active Directory Users and Computers**, you will see that **John Smith** has now been created as a **User** account. There aren't many properties that exist within this account, as it is pretty simple, but it will work in order to get a new user up and running:

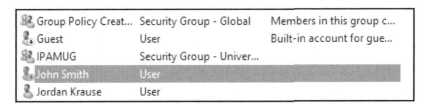

4. Now let's create another new user, this time adding some additional parameters to our code in order to populate more of the typical user information. You may have also noticed that our new **John Smith** user account is currently disabled—this happens automatically when you create a new user account but do not populate a password. So, we will add in some more information, up to the first name and surname. We will also specify a couple of additional parameters in order to make sure the account is enabled and to require that the user changes their password during their initial login:

```
New-ADUser - Name "Jase Robertson" -UserPrincipalName
"jrobertson@mydomain.local" - SamAccountName "jrobertson"  -
GivenName "Jase" -Surname "Robertson" -DisplayName  "Jase
Robertson" -AccountPassword (Read-Host -AsSecureString
"AccountPassword") -ChangePasswordAtLogon $true -Enabled $true
```

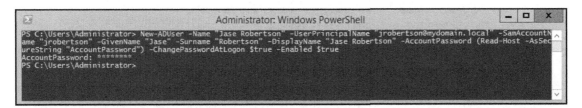

5. Open up **Active Directory Users and Computers** again and take a look at our new Jase Robertson user account. You can see that the account is enabled and ready for use, and it has much more information populated inside the account:

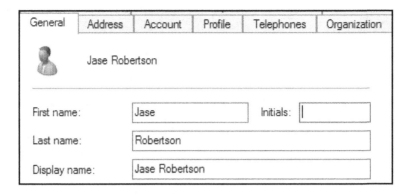

6. Move over to the **Account** tab and you will also see the box is now checked for **User must change password at next logon**, just like we specified in our PowerShell command:

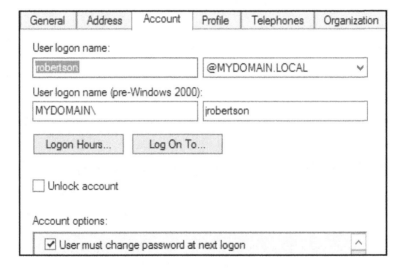

How it works...

By using PowerShell, we are able to create new Active Directory user accounts right from a command interface, rather than logging into a server and launching the graphical interface in order to accomplish this common task. Can your `New-ADUser` commands become extremely lengthy in order to populate all of the attributes you want to include? Yes. However, can saving and running a PowerShell script that utilizes `New-ADUser` cmdlet save you time in the long run? Absolutely! It might take a few minutes of thought and testing in order to get your script to the point where it populates the information that you would like, but once you have created and saved that script, it can be modified and run quickly in the future in order to create new accounts. There is even a way to utilize the `New-ADUser` cmdlet to copy properties from an existing user account while it sets up the new one, which may also help to save you some time and energy on new user account creations.

See also

Make sure to check out the following TechNet link. This page lists all of the possible parameters and syntax that you might want to run alongside your `New-ADUser` cmdlet script. There are a ton of options:

- `http://technet.microsoft.com/en-us/library/ee617253.aspx`

Using PowerShell to view system uptime

I find myself constantly checking servers to figure out what time they last restarted. Usually, this is part of troubleshooting something in order to figure out whether the server rebooted as a planned action or if something went wrong and it restarted on its own during a non-standard time. For years, I had launched Event Viewer, waited for the System logs to open, hoped that they weren't corrupted in some way, and then headed over to noon on the previous day to find the number of seconds that the system had been online. Then I'd pull out the calculator and do the math for how many days/hours that really was. Way too complicated! Thankfully, we can make calls into WMI objects with PowerShell, and there is an object in there that will tell us the last time the server started. With a few lines plugged into a `.ps1` script, we can create ourselves a nice little tool that will output the last time that a server booted. Let's give it a try.

Getting ready

We are using a Windows Server 2016 machine to build this script.

How to do it...

To build a script that shows us the last system boot time, perform the following steps:

1. Launch PowerShell ISE as an Administrator.
2. Open up a new script file and input the following line:

```
Get-WmiObject -Class Win32_OperatingSystem -ComputerName
localhost | Select-Object -Property LastBootUpTime
```

Untitled1.ps1* ✕

```
1   Get-WmiObject -Class Win32_OperatingSystem -ComputerName localhost |
2   Select-Object -Property LastBootUpTime
```

```
PS C:\Users\Administrator> Get-WmiObject -Class Win32_OperatingSystem -Compu

LastBootUpTime
--------------
20160517122955.129194-420


PS C:\Users\Administrator>
```

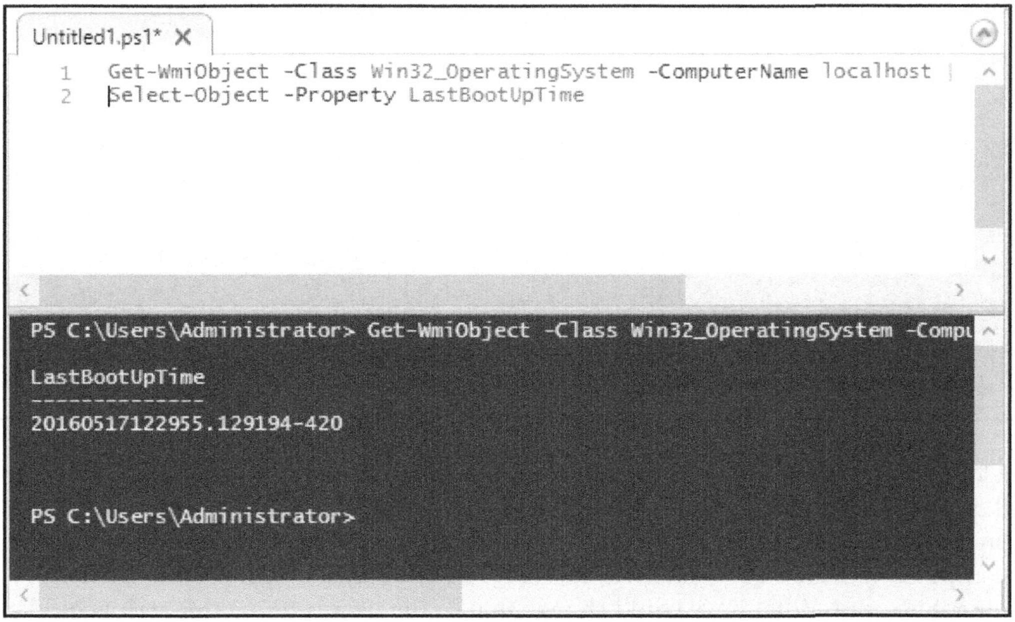

3. We have some data! It's kind of messy data, though. Maybe we can clean that up and make it a little more readable. With a couple of changes to our `Select-Object` code, we can change the header for this data to something more friendly, as well as changing the output of the date and time so it's way easier on the eyes:

```
Get-WmiObject -Class Win32_OperatingSystem -ComputerName
localhost | Select-Object -Property @{n="Last Boot Time";e=
{[Management.ManagementDateTimeConverter]::ToDateTime
($_.LastBootUpTime)}}
```

```
Untitled1.ps1* X
  1   Get-WmiObject -Class Win32_OperatingSystem -ComputerName localhost |
  2  Select-Object -Property @{n="Last Boot Time";
  3   e={[Management.ManagementDateTimeConverter]::ToDateTime($_.LastBootUpTime)}}
```

```
PS C:\Users\Administrator> Get-WmiObject -Class Win32_OperatingSystem -ComputerName localhos
Select-Object -Property @{n="Last Boot Time";
e={[Management.ManagementDateTimeConverter]::ToDateTime($_.LastBootUpTime)}}

Last Boot Time
--------------
5/17/2016 12:29:55 PM


PS C:\Users\Administrator>
```

That looks much better. At this point, I would say that this script is ready to be saved and used on any individual machine, and it would quickly give you the output you are looking for on that particular server. But, as you can see in the code, we are currently hardcoding the computer name to be `localhost`, the server or computer where we are currently running this script. What if we could change that so the user running this script could enter a different computer name? Maybe we could then use this script to execute a remote reach and find out when different servers last booted, without having to log into those servers?

Here is an example of doing just that. With a few changes to our code, we can require that the user inputs a computer name as a flag while running the script, and outputs two properties now. We will place an additional property identifier in there for the computer name itself so that it is clear to us in the output that the last boot time we are looking at the server name that we actually enter.

1. Use this for your script code:

```
Param(
  [Parameter(Mandatory=$true)][string]$ServerName
  )
Get-WmiObject -Class Win32_OperatingSystem -ComputerName
$ServerName | Select-Object -Property CSName,@{n="Last Boot
   Time";
e={[Management.ManagementDateTimeConverter]::
ToDateTime($_.LastBootUpTime)}}
```

2. Now when we run this script, we are asked to input the server name that we are trying to query:

```
Untitled1.ps1* X
 1  ⊟param(
 2        [Parameter(Mandatory=$true)][string]$ServerName
 3    |  )
 4
 5        Get-WmiObject -Class Win32_OperatingSystem -ComputerName $ServerName |
 6  ⊟     Select-Object -Property CSName.@{n="Last Boot Time";
 7    |    e={[Management.ManagementDateTimeConverter]::ToDateTime($_.LastBootUpTime)}}


PS C:\Users\Administrator> param(
    [Parameter(Mandatory=$true)][string]$ServerName
    )

    Get-WmiObject -Class Win32_OperatingSystem -ComputerName $ServerName |
    Select-Object -Property CSName.@{n="Last Boot Time";
    e={[Management.ManagementDateTimeConverter]::ToDateTime($_.LastBootUpTime)}}
cmdlet   at command pipeline position 1
Supply values for the following parameters:
ServerName: |
```

3. Go ahead and type `localhost` and you will receive the same boot time information as before, but now you see that we have a new column that shows us the server's name as well:

```
CSName Last Boot Time
------ --------------
DC1    5/17/2016 12:29:55 PM
```

4. Try running the script again, but this time enter the name of a remote server when it asks for **ServerName**. I will try to query our WEB1 web server. You should now see the last boot time output for that particular server with its name in the left column:

```
Untitled1.ps1* X
1  □param(
2         [Parameter(Mandatory=$true)][string]$ServerName
3         )
4
5         Get-WmiObject -Class Win32_OperatingSystem -ComputerName $ServerName |
6  □      Select-Object -Property CSName,@{n="Last Boot Time";
7         e={[Management.ManagementDateTimeConverter]::ToDateTime($_.LastBootUpTime)}}
```

```
      e={[Management.ManagementDateTimeConverter]::ToDateTime($_.LastBootUpTime)}}
cmdlet   at command pipeline position 1
Supply values for the following parameters:
ServerName: web1

CSName Last Boot Time
------ --------------
WEB1   5/17/2016 1:12:51 PM


PS C:\Users\Administrator> |
```

How it works...

In this recipe, we created a fun little script that asks for a server name and outputs the last boot information for the server entered. One of PowerShell's greatest attributes is its ability to grab information, both locally on the machine where you are running the script and on remote machines. This saves time, since you don't have to log into those servers to accomplish tasks, and makes your work environment more efficient.

One note on this particular script that we created, you don't have to run it as a first step and then take a second step in order to enter the server name. You are able to place the ServerName variable into your initial command when you launch the script. For example, open PowerShell and input the following command to launch the script:

```
.'Check Boot Time.ps1' -ServerName DC1
```

This will launch the script and automatically input DC1 as the server that it is checking, instead of stopping to ask you for input.

Internet Information Services 3

Websites and web services are used for everything these days. With the evolution of Cloud, we are accessing more and more via web browsers than we ever have before. The cloud can mean very different things to different people, but what I see most commonly in Enterprise is the creation of private clouds. This generally means a collection of web servers that are being used to serve up web applications for the company's user population to work from. Sometimes, the private cloud is onsite in a company's data center; sometimes it is in a co-location; and sometimes it is a combination of local data center and a true cloud web service provider such as Azure. Whatever defines a private cloud for you, one variable is the same. Your cloud includes web servers that need to be managed and administered.

For any Microsoft-centric shop, your web servers should be running Windows Server with the **Internet Information Services (IIS)** role installed. IIS is the website platform in Windows Server 2016, and with it we can run any kind of website or web service that we need. The hope for this collection of recipes is to give you a solid foundation to understand the way that websites work within IIS. Even if you don't normally set up new web services, you may very well have to troubleshoot one. Becoming familiar with the console and options, and just understanding the parts and pieces, can be hugely beneficial to anyone administering servers in a Windows environment. In this chapter, we will cover following recipes:

- Installing the Web Server role with PowerShell
- Launching your first website
- Changing the port on which your website runs
- Adding encryption to your website
- Using a Certificate Signing Request to acquire your SSL certificate
- Moving an SSL certificate from one server to another
- Rebinding your renewed certificates automatically
- Hosting multiple websites on your IIS server
- Using host headers to manage multiple websites on a single IP address

Introduction

We are going to assume, for most tasks in this chapter, that the role for IIS is already installed on the web server. This role is specifically called Web Server (IIS) in the list of roles, and there are numerous additional features that we can add to IIS. For all of our recipes, we only need the defaults added, the ones that are selected automatically when installing the role. That role installation is the only thing a Windows Server 2016 box needs in order to serve up web pages to users, other than a little bit of knowledge of how to get the site doing what you want it to do. In order to get the role installed properly, make sure to stop by the *Installing the Web Server role with PowerShell* recipe in order to put that component into place. Let's get familiar with some of the common tasks in IIS.

Installing the Web Server role with PowerShell

If you haven't started using PowerShell to accomplish some of your regular Windows Server tasks, do it now! PowerShell can be used in Windows Server 2016 to accomplish any task or configuration inside the operating system. I am a huge fan of using the keyboard instead of the mouse in any circumstance, and saving scripts that can be used over and over to save time in the future.

In this recipe, we are going to explore the `Install-WindowsFeature` cmdlet, which can be used to add a role or roles to your Server 2016. Since we are discussing IIS in this chapter, let's take our newly created web server and use PowerShell to place the Web Server (IIS) role onto it.

Getting ready

There is a new Windows Server 2016 web server in our environment called WEB2. Let's use PowerShell on this machine in order to install the IIS role.

How to do it...

To add the Web Server (IIS) role to WEB2 via PowerShell, follow these steps:

1. Log in to WEB2 and open a PowerShell prompt; make sure to run it as administrator.

2. All we have to do is run the proper cmdlet specifying the role name, but the specific name of our role evades me. Well, not really, but I thought this would be a good opportunity to explore another command that will help us see a list of the available roles to be installed. Type the following command to see the list of roles:

```
Get-WindowsFeature
```

3. Whoa! There's a big list of all the roles and features that can be installed on this server. Scrolling up, I can see Web Server (IIS) in the list, and it looks like the role name is Web-Server. I am going to keep that name in mind, and since we have the ability to install multiple items at the same time, I am also going to note Web-Common-Http in order to install the common HTTP features when I install the role:

```
[ ] Volume Activation Services              VolumeActivation
[ ] Web Server (IIS)                        Web-Server
    [ ] Web Server                          Web-WebServer
        [ ] Common HTTP Features            Web-Common-Http
            [ ] Default Document            Web-Default-Doc
            [ ] Directory Browsing          Web-Dir-Browsing
            [ ] HTTP Errors                 Web-Http-Errors
            [ ] Static Content              Web-Static-Content
            [ ] HTTP Redirection            Web-Http-Redirect
            [ ] WebDAV Publishing           Web-DAV-Publishing
        [ ] Health and Diagnostics          Web-Health
```

4. Now we need to build out the PowerShell command to install these two items:

```
Install-WindowsFeature Web-Server,Web-Common-Http,Web-Mgmt-
Console -Restart
```

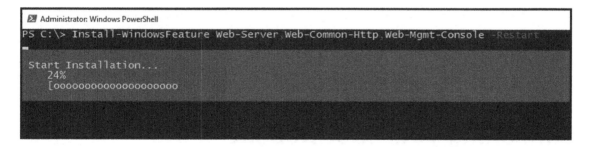

```
Administrator: Windows PowerShell
PS C:\> Install-WindowsFeature Web-Server,Web-Common-Http,Web-Mgmt-Console -Restart

Start Installation...
   24%
   [oooooooooooooooooooooo
```

5. Installation succeeded! Just to double-check it for the sake of our recipe, if we navigate through the GUI to see the installed roles and features, we can see that the items we configured via PowerShell are fully installed:

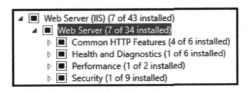

How it works...

We can use the `Install-WindowsFeature` cmdlet in PowerShell to easily add roles and features to our servers. This one can save a lot of time compared to running through these options in the graphical wizards. For example, if you had a group of new servers that all needed to accomplish the same task, and therefore needed the same set of roles installed, you could build out one single command to install those roles and run it on each server. No need to launch Server Manager at all.

See also

Here are some links to additional TechNet documentation on adding roles to servers, and specifically for the `Install-WindowsFeature` cmdlet. Make sure to familiarize yourself with all of the available options. Once you start using this command, I doubt you will go back to Server Manager!

- http://technet.microsoft.com/en-us/library/cc732263.aspx#BKMK_ powershell
- http://technet.microsoft.com/en-us/library/jj205467.aspx

Launching your first website

Seems like a pretty logical first step; let's get a website started! Actually, you already have one, but it's pretty useless at the moment. As soon as you finished installing the IIS role, a standard website was started automatically so that you can verify everything is working as it should. Now we want to replace that default website with one of our own so that we can make some real use of this new server.

Getting ready

We will be accomplishing all work from our new Server 2016 web server. This one does happen to be domain joined, but that is not a requirement. You would be able to launch a website on a standalone, workgroup joined server just as easily.

How to do it...

Follow these steps to start your first website on this new IIS web server:

1. Open **Server Manager** and drop down the **Tools** menu. Then click on **Internet Information Services (IIS) Manager**.
2. In the left-hand window pane, expand the name of your server and click on the **Sites** folder.
3. Right-click on **Default Web Site** and navigate to **Manage Website** | **Stop**. This will stop that automatically created website from running and getting in the way of the new website that we are about to create:

4. Before we create our new website, we will need to create an HTML webpage file that will run when users browse to the new site. Let's leave IIS Manager open for a minute and switch over to File Explorer. Browse to `C:\inetpub`. This is sort of the home folder that IIS creates and can be a good starting point for building your website. You do not have to create your new page within this folder, you could certainly set one up in another location, or even on a different drive altogether.

5. Create a new folder called `NewWebsite`, or whatever you want it to be called.

6. Inside this new folder, we are going to create a new file called `Default.htm`. To do this, I usually right-click and choose to create a new text file, and name this file `Default.txt`. Then I either adjust **Folder Options** so that I can see and modify file extensions, or I simply open up a **Command Prompt** window and rename the file that way. However you do it, make sure that your `Default.txt` gets changed to `Default.htm` as the final filename:

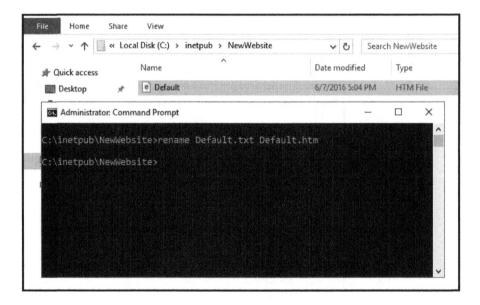

7. Now edit your new `Default.htm` file with Notepad or another text editing tool and enter some text. Thankfully, modern web browsers will properly display a page based on some plain text, so that we don't have to input valid HTML code. If you know how to program in HTML, even better, though I doubt you would be reading this particular recipe. Or maybe you have a preconfigured webpage file or set of files from a software installation; you could place those into this folder as well. I am going to simply enter some text in that file, which says, `Congratulations, you are viewing our new website!`.

8. Head back over to IIS, and let's get our site rolling. Right-click on the `Sites` folder and choose **Add Website...**.

9. Input a site name, which is just a descriptive name for your own purposes to identify the site in IIS.

10. For the **Physical path**, choose our new website location, which is as follows: `C:\inetpub\NewWebsite`.

11. If you are running multiple IP addresses on this web server and want to dedicate this new site to only run on a particular IP address, you can choose it from the **IP address** field. Otherwise, if you are running a single IP or if you want our new site to work on all IPs configured on this system, leave it set to **All Unassigned**:

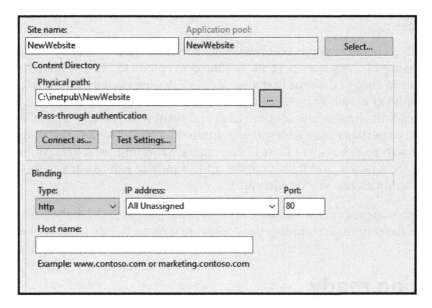

12. Click **OK**.

13. From another computer on the network, open up Internet Explorer and browse to `http://<webserver>`. For our particular example, we will go to `http://web2`:

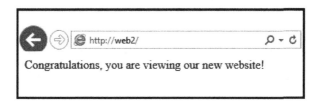

How it works...

Starting a new website is perhaps the simplest task that can be accomplished in IIS, but it portrays the core functionality of this role. The purpose of running IIS in the first place is to publish websites. It is important to understand the location of this task and the places that you may have to reach inside the filesystem in order to modify or create websites of your own. Not everything is done from within the IIS Management window.

Changing the port on which your website runs

Normally, whenever you access a website, it is running on port 80 or 443. Any normal HTTP request travels over port 80, and the encrypted HTTPS uses port 443. Inside IIS, it is very easy to change the port that a website is listening on if you need to do so. Probably the most common reason to institute a port change on a website is to keep it hidden. Maybe you have an administrative site of some kind and want to make sure that nobody stumbles across it, or perhaps your web server is limited on IP addresses, and you need to turn on another web page but all of your IPs are already running sites. You could utilize a different port for the new site and then have the opportunity to run two (or more) sites using the same IP address, one site on each port.

Whatever your reason for wanting to change the port that a website runs on, let's walk through the steps to accomplish this task so that it can be one more tool added to your belt.

Getting ready

We have a Windows Server 2016 server online that has the IIS role installed. There is already a website running on this server. Currently, it is using port 80 by default, but we want to change that port to 81 and test accessing it from a client computer.

How to do it...

Here are the steps needed to change your website listener port:

1. Open **Internet Information Services (IIS) Manager** from inside the **Tools** menu of Server Manager.

2. In the left-hand window pane, expand the name of your web server and click on the **Sites** folder.
3. Right-click on your website and choose **Bindings....**:

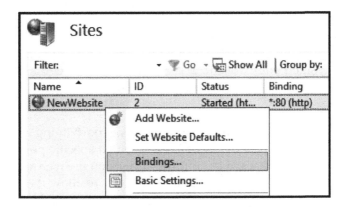

4. Choose the **http** binding that currently displays port **80** and click on the **Edit...** button.
5. Change the **Port** field to 81. This is just for our example, of course. You could enter any valid port number in this field that isn't otherwise in use on this server.
6. Click **OK**, then **Close**.
7. The port is immediately changed on your website. It is no longer listening on port 80. Let's test this by moving to a client computer on our network and opening Internet Explorer.
8. Try browsing to the old website address, http://web2:

This page can't be displayed

9. Whoops! I guess that isn't going to work anymore. Instead, we need to include our specific port in the URL from now on. Let's try http://web2:81:

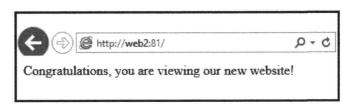

How it works...

We can easily adjust the port that is used to access a website inside IIS by making one simple adjustment. After changing the port number in our website's bindings, the site immediately changes over to listening on the new port and is no longer active on the old port. Instead of changing the port, you could also add an additional binding into that same screen in order to get the website to respond from multiple ports at the same time. For example, if you wanted your website to run both HTTP for regular access and HTTPS for encrypted access to pages with sensitive information, you could create bindings for both port 80 and port 443.

One note of importance when changing your website port; doing so means your web links for accessing the website will now have to include that specific port number at the end. Also, if you are running firewalls in your network or on the web server itself, it is possible that you will need to adjust settings on those firewalls to allow the new port to be allowed safe passage.

Adding encryption to your website

Using websites to pass data around the Internet is a staple of technology as we know it today. Installing even the simplest new tool or system will probably require you to download software or an update, or to register your information with a website. As an IT professional, I hope that you are familiar with HTTP versus HTTPS websites and the importance of distinguishing between the two. But now that we have a website running, how can we enable HTTPS on it so that we can protect this data that is traversing back and forth between our web server and the client computers?

It is typically the web developer's job to tell a website when to call for HTTPS, so you shouldn't have to worry too much about the actual content of the website. As the server administrator, however, you need to make sure that once HTTPS is called for on the website, your web server is capable of processing that traffic appropriately.

Getting ready

We are running a Server 2016 web server from which we will accomplish this task. There is a simple website currently running inside IIS on this server. Part of our recipe will be choosing an SSL certificate that we want to run on our website, so this recipe assumes that the certificate is already installed on your server. If you need assistance with the acquisition of the certificate itself, please refer to the *Using a Certificate Signing Request to acquire your SSL certificate* recipe.

How to do it...

To configure your website for HTTPS traffic, follow these steps:

1. Launch **Internet Information Services (IIS) Manager** from the **Tools** menu inside Server Manager.
2. In the left-hand window pane, expand your web server name and click on the **Sites** folder.
3. Right-click on your website and choose **Bindings...**:

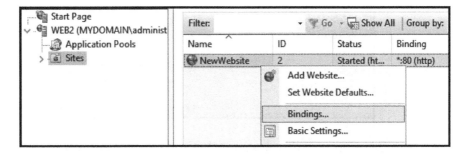

Since it is a new website, you can see that there is only one binding listed currently. This binding is for port 80, which makes it an HTTP-only website. If you currently tried to access this site via HTTPS, it would fail. The port for HTTPS is 443, and so we need to add a new binding that uses port 443. A mistake that I have watched new admins make is to edit this existing binding and change it from 80 to 443. This will cause the website to only listen on port 443, or rather to only accept requests via HTTPS. This may be desirable in some instances, but not most. You generally want the website to respond to both HTTP and HTTPS requests.

4. Go ahead and click the **Add...** button.

5. Change the **Type** field to **https**. You will notice that the **Port** field changes to 443 automatically.

6. If you only want this new binding to work on a particular IP address, choose it now. Otherwise, leave it set to **All Unassigned** to cause this new listener to be active on all IP addresses that exist on our server.

7. Select the **SSL certificate** that you want IIS to use for authenticating requests to this website. HTTPS traffic is only encrypted and guaranteed to be safe from prying eyes because the tunnel is being validated by an SSL certificate that is specific to your website name. You must have an SSL certificate installed on the server so that you can choose it from the list here in order to create an HTTPS binding:

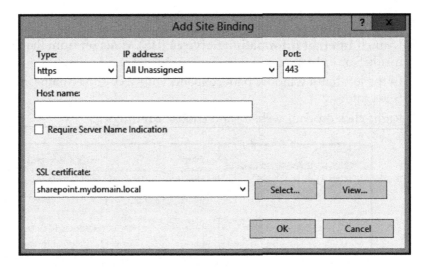

8. Click **OK**, then click **Close**. Your HTTPS binding is now active on this website.

How it works...

In this recipe, we used the IIS management console to add a second binding to our new website. This new binding is for accepting HTTPS traffic. We intend to run parts of this website as HTTP, and some more sensitive pages as HTTPS. Therefore, we created a second binding, enabling both HTTP and HTTPS traffic to flow successfully to and from this site. During the course of this recipe, we needed to choose the SSL certificate that the website is going to use in order to validate the HTTPS traffic that is coming in. There was already an SSL certificate installed on the server for our website; we simply had to choose it from the list.

Using a Certificate Signing Request to acquire your SSL certificate

When publishing a website to the Internet, it is generally a best practice to use an SSL certificate on the website that you acquired from a public Certification Authority (CA). These are the big certificate issuing entities such as Entrust, Verisign, Digicert, GoDaddy, and so on. It is possible to use your own internal PKI infrastructure to issue SSL certificates that can be exposed to the outside world, but it can be difficult to set up the certificate infrastructure appropriately and securely. As cheap as SSL certificates are, it is worth the investment to have the security of knowing that the certificate you are running on your website is the one and only certificate of its kind, and that nobody else has a chance to get their hands on a copy of your certificate and spoof your website. Modern browsers also have a pre-built list of the public CAs that they trust; this makes using a certificate from one of those public entities even more beneficial, because your user's browsers will automatically trust those certificates without any additional work on the client side.

It is easy enough to log in to one of these CA's websites and purchase a new certificate, but then comes the tricky part. Once purchased, you need to walk through some steps and enter information about your certificate. Easy enough; it asks you for some company information and the name that you plan to use for your site, of course. Then it asks for your **Certificate Signing Request (CSR)** and gives you either a very large empty text box to paste it into or an upload function where you can upload your CSR directly to them. This is the place where I have watched many new admins struggle to find traction on their next step.

A CSR is a file that must be created on your web server. It contains information that the CA uses when it creates your certificate. When they do this, it binds the certificate to the information in the CSR, ensuring that your certificate is built specifically for your web server. Here, we are going to generate a CSR together, so that you are prepared to handle that screen when you come across it.

Getting ready

We are going to use IIS that is running on our Server 2016 web server to generate a CSR. This server is the only piece of infrastructure that we need running for this task.

How to do it...

In order to request a new certificate from a public CA, you will need to spin out a CSR on your web server. Here are the steps to do so:

1. Open **Internet Information Services (IIS) Manager**.
2. Click on the name of your server in the left-hand window pane.
3. Double-click on the **Server Certificates** applet. This will display currently installed certificates on your server:

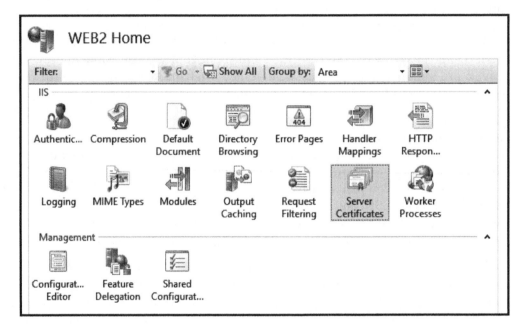

4. Click on the action near the right of your screen that says **Create Certificate Request...**.
5. Populate **Common name** with the DNS name that your website will be running on. This is the name that users will type into their browsers in order to access this site.
6. **Organization** is the name of your company or organization. Typically, this information needs to match whatever is on file with the CA, so take a minute to check another certificate that you might have already and make sure to type in the same info.
7. The **Organizational unit** can be anything you desire. I often just type the word Web.

8. Type in your **City/locality** and **State/province** to finish out this screen. Make sure to spell out the whole word of your state, for example, California. They tend to dislike abbreviations:

9. Click **Next**.
10. Increase your **Bit length** to at least **2048**. This is typically considered to be the new minimum standard in the industry:

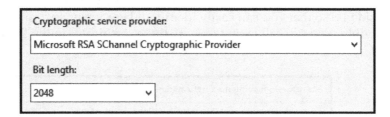

11. Click **Next**.
12. Type a location and name where you want to store your new CSR. Usually, you set this into a text (.txt) file. Make sure to specify the full filename, including the extension. I have found that if you do not, the file disappears into neverland:

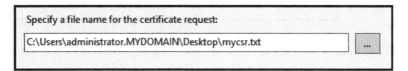

13. Click **Finish** and go take a look at that new file. It will look like a big mess of letters and numbers, which is normal!

14. Now you can proceed to your public CA's web interface and use this new CSR during the official request for a new SSL certificate. When prompted, paste the contents of the CSR file into their system. This is the last time you will need that CSR.

 Each authority handles this process differently, but they are all generally done through a website, with a series of steps that you walk through. Many CAs will allow you to generate a 15 or 30-day trial certificate so that you can test this without cost.

15. After the CA validates your request and your CSR, they will issue you a link where you can download your new certificate. Go ahead and download that file, and copy it onto your web server.

16. Once the certificate file is on your server, you need to import it into IIS. Head back into the **Server Certificates** section and this time click on **Complete Certificate Request....**

17. Specify the newly downloaded certificate file and input the **Friendly name** field if you choose. This is a descriptive name that you can give to this new certificate inside IIS so that you can easily identify it later when assigning it to a website binding. You typically want to store these certificates in the **Personal** store, as is set by default:

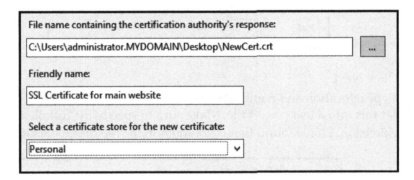

18. Click **OK**, and that's it! Your new certificate is installed and ready to use.

How it works...

In this recipe, we requested a new SSL certificate from our favorite public Certification Authority. In order to receive a certificate from them, we had to issue a CSR from our web server. Once we have our CSR generated, we simply copy and paste it into the web interface for our CA entity and they give us a new certificate based on that CSR. Once downloaded, the new certificate file can be imported back into the web server, where it is ready for use by our own website.

One note of importance; after you install the new certificate on your server, double-click on the certificate to open it up. You want to make sure that you have a message displaying on the main page of your certificate properties that says **You have a private key that corresponds to this certificate**. This will display near the bottom of the **General** tab of the certificate. If you do not see this message, something did not work correctly with the CSR and you will probably have to start the process over to request another new copy of the certificate. Having a private key that corresponds to your SSL certificate is critical to getting your website working properly.

Moving an SSL certificate from one server to another

There are multiple reasons why you may need to move or copy an SSL certificate from one web server to another. If you have purchased a wildcard certificate for your network, you are probably going to use that same certificate on a lot of different servers, as it can be used to validate multiple websites and DNS names. Even if you are using singularly named certificates, you may be turning on multiple web servers to host the same site, to be set up in some sort of load-balanced fashion. In this case, you will also need the same SSL certificate on each of the web servers, as they could all potentially be accepting traffic from clients.

When moving or copying a certificate from one server to another, there is definitely a right way and a wrong way to go about it. Let's spend a little bit of time copying a certificate from one server to another so that you can become familiar with this task.

Getting ready

We have two Server 2016 boxes online in our environment. These are both destined to be web servers hosting the same website. IIS has been installed on both. The SSL certificate that we require has been installed on the primary server. We now need to export the certificate from there and import it successfully onto our second server.

How to do it...

Follow these steps to copy a certificate from one server to another:

1. On your primary web server, launch **Internet Information Services (IIS) Manager** from the **Tools** menu of Server Manager.
2. Click on the name of your server in the left-hand window pane.
3. Double-click on the **Server Certificates** applet to view the certificates currently installed on this system.
4. For our example, I am using a wildcard certificate that has been installed on this server. Right-click on the certificate and choose **Export...**:

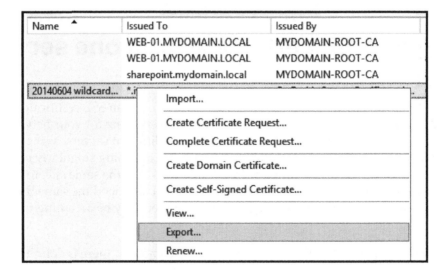

5. Choose a location to store this exported file and enter a password that will be used to protect the file:

6. Clicking **OK** will create a `PFX` file and place it onto your Desktop (or wherever you told it to save). Now copy this `PFX` file over to your secondary web server.

7. Open up the IIS Management console on the second server and navigate to the same **Server Certificates** location.

8. Right-click in the center pane and choose **Import....** Alternatively, you could choose the **Import...** action from the right-hand window pane.

9. Browse to the location of your certificate and input the password that you used to protect the `PFX` file.

10. Before clicking **OK**, decide whether or not you want this certificate to be exportable from this secondary server. Sometimes this is desirable if you plan to have to export the certificate again in the future. If you do not have a reason to do that, go ahead and uncheck this box. Unchecking **Allow this certificate to be exported** helps to limit the places where you have certificates floating around the network. The more you have out there that are potentially exportable, the more chance you have of one getting out of your hands:

11. Once you click **OK**, your certificate should now be installed and visible inside the IIS window.

12. Double-click on the certificate and check over the properties to make sure everything looks correct. Make sure that you see the message across the bottom that says **You have a private key that corresponds to this certificate**. If that message is missing, something didn't work properly during your export and the private key was somehow not included in the certificate export that you did. You will have to revisit the primary server and export again to make sure that the certificate on the secondary server does contain private key information, or it will not work properly:

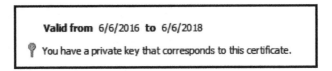

How it works...

We used the IIS management console to export and import an SSL certificate, which is a pretty straightforward and simple task to do once you understand the process. The critical part is making sure that your export includes the private key information. If it does not, the certificate will not be able to validate traffic properly. Using IIS to accomplish this task is the best way to move certificates. You could also make use of the MMC snap-in for certificates, but it is a little more complicated. If you try to use that console, you will be asked whether or not you want to export the private key. The default option is set to **No, do not export the private key**. It is a common mistake to leave that setting in place and wonder later why the certificate doesn't work properly on other servers where you have installed it. You must make sure to select the option **Yes, export the private key**.

Rebinding your renewed certificates automatically

Certificates expire; this is just a simple fact of life. Most often, I find that companies purchase SSL certificates on a short-term basis, usually for only one year. This means that every year, each certificate needs to be renewed. However, downloading a new copy of the certificate and installing it onto your web server is not enough to make it continue working. Simply putting the new certificate into place on the server does not mean that IIS is going to start using the new one to validate traffic on your website. Even if you delete the old certificate, there is no action that has been taken inside IIS to tell it that this new certificate that suddenly appeared is the one that it should start using as the binding for your site. So we have always had to make this additional change manually. Every time you replace a certificate, you also go into IIS and change the binding on the website. This seems particularly painful when you have the certificate renewal automated through something such as Autoenrollment. You may mistakenly think that you are covered in the future and no longer have to do anything to renew your certificates because they will be renewed at the server level automatically. But alas, this is not true; up until now we have still always had to go into IIS and change the binding by hand. Fear not, the future is here...

The IIS team has made a simple but powerful change to help this problem in the new version of IIS that ships with Windows Server 2016. In fact, this function was available in Server 2012 R2 in its first iteration, but I still haven't seen anybody use it in the field, so for most folks, this is going to be brand new. This new feature called **Certificate Rebind**, when enabled, causes IIS to automatically recognize a new certificate installation, and to automatically rebind the appropriate website to use the new copy of the certificate instead of the expiring one. Let's take a look at the interface so that you know how to turn this option on and off. We will also take a little look under the hood so that you can understand how this functionality works.

Getting ready

This work will be accomplished on our Windows Server 2016 web server. We have IIS installed and have an HTTPS website running with an SSL certificate already bound to the site.

How to do it...

Follow these steps to enable Certificate Rebind on your IIS web server:

1. Open **Internet Information Services (IIS) Manager** from inside the **Tools** menu of Server Manager.
2. In the left-hand window pane, click on the name of your web server.
3. Double-click on the **Server Certificates** applet.
4. In the right-hand window pane, click on the action called **Enable Automatic Rebind of Renewed Certificate**:

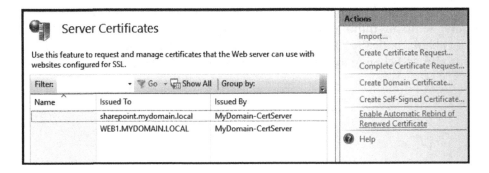

5. That's it! IIS has now been configured so that it will recognize the installation of a renewed certificate, and will rebind your website automatically to make use of the new certificate. Now let's take a little look at how this process actually works.

6. Use either Command Prompt or the **Start** screen to launch `Taskschd.msc`. This is the **Windows Task Scheduler**.

7. In the left-hand pane, navigate to **Task Scheduler Library** | **Microsoft** | **Windows** | **CertificateServicesClient**:

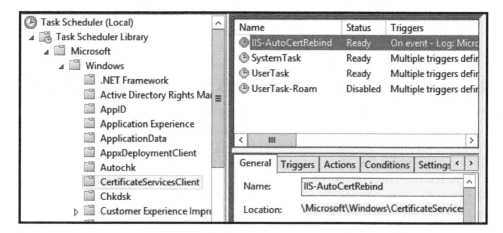

8. You can see a scheduled task listed here that is called **IIS-AutoCertRebind**. This is the magic of Certificate Rebind. When a certificate gets added or renewed on your Server 2016 system, an event is logged. When this event is logged, this scheduled task picks it up and uses the information that it has from IIS about the certificates to rebind the websites onto the new certificates.

9. If you head back into IIS and click on the **Action** for **Disable Automatic Rebind of Renewed Certificate**, you will notice that our scheduled task disappears from the list.

How it works...

Certificate Rebind is a really simple action to enable inside IIS, but it can make all the difference to whether you have a good or bad day at the office. When enabled, this feature builds a scheduled task inside Windows that triggers the commands to bind our IIS website to its new certificate. This task is triggered by an event that is logged in Windows when our new certificate is installed or renewed. With Certificate Rebind enabled and the configuration of your certificate distribution set to happen automatically through Autoenrollment, you can now have a truly automated certificate renewal system inside your network!

Hosting multiple websites on your IIS server

Spinning up a web server, implementing the IIS role, and hosting a website are great first steps. Depending on the size and importance of your website, you may even require multiple web servers running that will serve up exact copies of the same website and have load balancing configured between the multiple web servers. On the other hand, it is probably more likely that your website will actually be an underutilization of your server's resources, rather than an overutilization, and so you have now created a new web server hosting a single website, and it's really not being taxed at all. Is there a way that we can make use of that extra hardware that is currently sitting idle? Perhaps you have additional websites or web services that need to be turned on, for which you were planning to spin up multiple servers. The good news is that IIS is capable of hosting many different websites at the same time. We can take that underutilized server and create additional website listeners on it so that you can serve up multiple web pages from the same physical server.

There are a couple of different ways that we can host multiple websites on the same IIS server at the same time, through the use of multiple ports or multiple IP addresses. Let's take a minute and test both avenues.

Getting ready

We are going to use IIS on our WEB1 server today in order to host multiple websites. We will also need access to DNS in order to create names for these websites.

How to do it...

Follow these steps to host multiple websites on the same IIS server:

1. First, we need to create some sites that will be served up by IIS. Inside my `c:\inetpub` folder, I am simply creating four new folders. Inside each folder will be a simple `Default.htm` file that contains some text. This way I can serve up these different web pages on different sites inside IIS, and later browse to them individually to prove that IIS is serving up all of the different web pages:

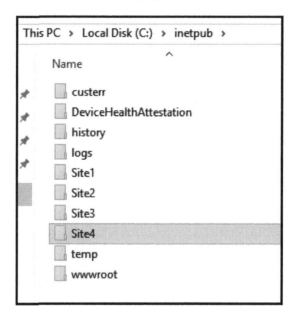

2. Now open up **Internet Information Services (IIS) Manager** and browse to the **Sites** folder. Right-click on **Sites** and choose **Add Website...** four different times to walk through the process of creating your four new websites. For each site, make sure to choose the appropriate folder on the hard drive for serving up the correct page.

3. At this point in time, we only have one IP address on our web server. So in order to allow IIS to host multiple websites on this single IP address, we are going to take the approach of having each website run on its own port number. When you configure the **Add Website** screen, identify a unique port number under the **Binding** session for each site. This will permit all four websites to run at the same time using the same IP address, because each site will be running on a unique port number:

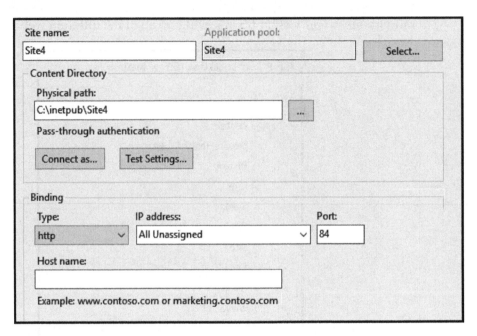

4. Now you can see that all four of our websites are started, and each is running on its own port number:

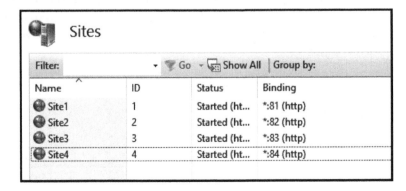

5. Client computers in the network can now browse the following links and successfully see the four different web pages being served up by our IIS server:

   - `http://web1:81`
   - `http://web1:82`
   - `http://web1:83`
   - `http://web1:84`

6. Requiring the users to type in a specific port number when they want to access websites isn't something they are going to appreciate, so let's try hosting these four different websites on our WEB1 server in a different fashion. Instead of using different port numbers, we are now going to take the approach of hosting each website on its own unique IP address. In order to start that process, open up the NIC properties of the WEB1 server and plug in three additional IP addresses that we can use specifically for hosting these websites:

```
Ethernet adapter Ethernet:

   Connection-specific DNS Suffix  . :
   Link-local IPv6 Address . . . . . : fe80::79a1:f04f:406e:f589%3
   IPv4 Address. . . . . . . . . . . : 10.0.0.21
   Subnet Mask . . . . . . . . . . . : 255.255.255.0
   IPv4 Address. . . . . . . . . . . : 10.0.0.22
   Subnet Mask . . . . . . . . . . . : 255.255.255.0
   IPv4 Address. . . . . . . . . . . : 10.0.0.23
   Subnet Mask . . . . . . . . . . . : 255.255.255.0
   IPv4 Address. . . . . . . . . . . : 10.0.0.24
   Subnet Mask . . . . . . . . . . . : 255.255.255.0
   Default Gateway . . . . . . . . . :
```

7. Now back inside IIS, right-click on each of your websites and modify **Bindings...** so that each website is once again using the default port 80, but it is also running on its own unique IP address:

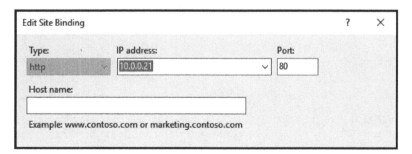

8. Once the four websites are each running on their own IP addresses, you can create DNS host records so that each site has a unique DNS name on the network as well. Simply point these four new DNS names to the corresponding IP address where the site is running, and your client computers can now access the websites via individual hostnames on the network:

   - `http://site1.mydomain.local`
   - `http://site2.mydomain.local`
   - `http://site3.mydomain.local`
   - `http://site4.mydomain.local`

Site1	Host (A)	10.0.0.21
Site2	Host (A)	10.0.0.22
Site3	Host (A)	10.0.0.23
Site4	Host (A)	10.0.0.24

How it works...

Whether you decide to host multiple websites on a single web server by splitting up access at the port level or the IP address level, it is important to know that you can push the limits of your web server a little bit by hosting multiple things at the same time. IIS is more than capable of handling this division of resources, and as long as your hardware is keeping up with the task, you can continue to grow vertically in this way and save the number of servers you have running, rather than having to grow out horizontally by installing server after server after server, as you begin to need additional web resources.

Using host headers to manage multiple websites on a single IP address

As we just saw, it is pretty straightforward to configure multiple websites inside IIS by assigning individual IP addresses for each site. It is common to run more than one site on a single web server, and so this sometimes means that your web servers have numerous IP addresses configured on them. However, sometimes this is not possible. For example, you may be working on a web server that is Internet facing and there is a restriction on the amount of available public IP addresses that can be used. In this case, you may run across the need to host multiple websites on a single IP address, but you don't want to force the users into having to type in specific port numbers in order to gain access to the right website.

This is where host headers come into play. Host headers can be configured on your websites so that the site responds to a particular request coming in from the client. These header requests can help the web server distinguish between traffic, directing users calling for websites to their appropriate site inside IIS. Let's work together to set up two websites inside IIS and force them to utilize the same IP address and port. We want everything to remain standard as far as the port goes, so we want them to both be able to utilize port 80, but we only have one IP address available to install on our web server.

Getting ready

The work will be accomplished from inside IIS on our Server 2016 web server. We will also utilize a client computer to test connectivity to the websites once we are finished setting them up.

How to do it...

To create two websites that share the same IP address and split traffic by using host headers, follow these steps:

1. On your web server, open up File Explorer and create a new folder called `C:\Websites`. Inside this folder, create two new folders and call them `Site1` and `Site2`.

2. Inside each folder, create a new `Default.htm` file. You should now have two different `Default.htm` files, one sitting inside the `Site1` folder, and one sitting inside the `Site2` folder. These will be our example websites.

3. Put some text inside each of those `Default.htm` files. Make sure that whatever text you write in them distinguishes between the websites so that we can know it is working properly when we test in a few minutes.

4. Open **Internet Information Services (IIS) Manager** from the **Tools** menu of Server Manager.

5. In the left-hand window pane, expand the name of your web server. Then right-click on the `Sites` folder, and choose **Add Website...**.

6. We are going to name our site `Site1` and choose our `C:\Websites\Site1` folder as the location for this website. I am also going to drop down the **IP address** field and specify the one and only IP address on this system so that we can prove host headers are working as they should. Remember, our intention is to get two websites running on this same IP address and port combination.

7. Here's the part that may be new territory for you, the **Host name** field. This is the DNS name that requests for this website will be coming in with. So whatever DNS name your users are going to type into their browser is the name that you need to enter here. We are going to use `mysite1.mydomain.local`:

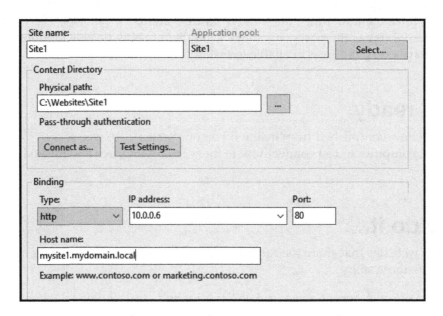

8. Click **OK**, and you have the first website up and running on the web server.

9. Now walk through the same process as above, but this time specify all of the information for Site2. We are going to choose the same **IP address** and **Port**, but we are going to specify a different name in the **Host name** field:

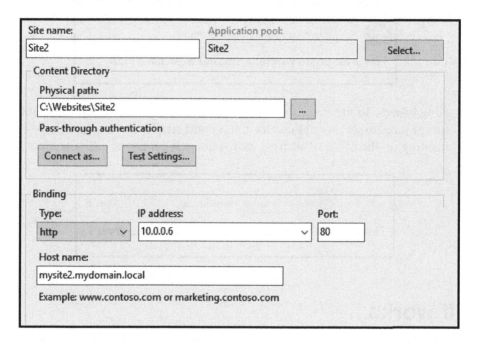

10. We now have two websites, both running on the same IP address and port on the same web server. Let's test to find out whether or not IIS is smart enough to distinguish between the sites when we try to browse these websites from our client computer.

Remember to create DNS records for these websites! You will need host records created for mysite1.mydomain.local and mysite2.mydomain.local, and they both need to be pointed at the IP address of the web server, which in our case is 10.0.0.6.

11. On a client computer, browse to `http://mysite1.mydomain.local`. You should see the text from the `Default.htm` file that we put into the `Site1` folder on the web server:

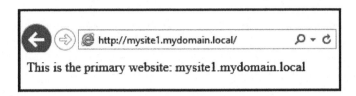

12. Now browse to `http://mysite2.mydomain.local`. We can see that the web server recognizes our request for the second site, and even though they are running on the same IP address, our request is sent over to the second website:

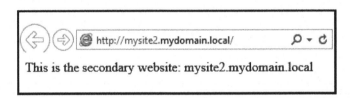

How it works...

When we set up websites inside IIS to utilize different host headers, it gives us the ability to publish multiple sites on the same IP address and port numbers. This can be very useful in cases where IP addresses are limited or where you don't want to configure multiple addresses onto the web server for any reason. IIS is capable of listening on the same IP and port for web requests coming into different host names and forwarding those requests on to the appropriate website based on the host header name that was requested by the client computer. It is important to note that requests for these web pages must come by the name for this to work properly; you cannot type the IP address of the website into the browser and expect it to work, since we are now sharing that IP address between two or more different sites.

4
Remote Desktop Services

Remote Desktop Services (RDS) is an outstanding way to provide users with access to applications and data, without those applications and data needing to reside on their local workstations. Formerly known as Terminal Services, this technology enables companies to retain control of all data and apps on centralized Remote Desktop servers, which users connect to from their workstations in order to access these items. There are two primary means of providing this information to users. The first is through a remote session, where users log into a **Remote Desktop Session Host (RDSH)** server and end up landing inside a session hosted on the server. This session looks and feels like a regular desktop computer to the user, as they have a full desktop and Start button and are able to launch any application available to them within that session. They are also able to save documents inside their session, keeping everything centralized. This is the most common flavor of RDS that I see used in the field and is where we will focus the majority of our administrative tasks that we discuss today.

A second way to provide data to users via RDS is *RemoteApp*. This is a neat function that is able to provide only the application itself remotely to the user's computer, rather than a full desktop session. This is a nice way to further restrict the access that is being provided to the user and simplifies the steps the user must take in order to access those resources.

An RDS environment has the potential to contain many servers, enough to fill its own book. Given that, let's work together to get a simple RDS environment online that you can start testing with, and provide you with knowledge of some common administrative tasks that will be useful in an environment like this.

In this chapter, you'll be taking a look at the following recipes:

- Building a single server Remote Desktop Services environment
- Adding an additional RDSH server to your RDS environment
- Installing applications on a Remote Desktop Session Host server
- Disabling the redirection of local resources
- Shadowing another session in RDS
- Installing a printer driver to use with redirection
- Removing an RD Session Host server from use for maintenance
- Publishing WordPad with RemoteApp
- Tracking user logins with Logon/Logoff scripts

Introduction

I would like to take a minute and describe the different parts and pieces that could potentially make up your RDS environment. We won't be covering the installation or use of all components that might be involved with a full RDS deployment, but you should at least be aware of the components and their intended functions:

- **Remote Desktop Session Host**: This is the most common type of RDS server, as it is the one hosting the programs and sessions that users connect to. Depending on the size of your environment, there may be many of these servers running concurrently.
- **Remote Desktop Connection Broker**: This is like the load balancer for RDS servers. It distributes users evenly across RDSH servers, and helps users to reconnect to existing sessions rather than creating fresh ones.
- **Remote Desktop Licensing**: This is responsible for managing the licenses that are required for RDS use in a network.
- **Remote Desktop Gateway**: This is a gateway device that can bring remote users out on the Internet into an RDS environment. For example, a user at home could utilize the connection provided by an RD Gateway in order to access work information.
- **Remote Desktop Web Access**: This enables users to access desktops and applications by using the local Start menu on their Windows 7, 8, or 10 computers. Users can also utilize this to access applications via a web browser.

- **Remote Desktop Virtualization Host**: This is a role that integrates with Hyper-V in order to provide virtual desktop sessions to users. The difference here is that resources given to those users are spun up from Hyper-V, rather than shared resources such as an RDSH.

Many of these roles can be placed together on a single server, which is what we will be doing in our recipe to bring a simple RDS environment online. As your deployment grows and you continue to add users and servers, it is generally a good idea to make these roles decentralized and redundant when possible.

Building a single server Remote Desktop Services environment

If you aren't coming into an environment where RDS is already up-and-running, it will be helpful to understand where the roles come from and how they are put into place. In this recipe, we are going to combine a number of Remote Desktop roles onto a single server so that we can take a look at that installation process. When we are finished, we should have an RDS server that will allow users to connect and utilize a Remote Desktop session.

Getting ready

We will be using a Windows Server 2016 machine to install the RDS roles. This server is already joined to our domain.

How to do it...

The following steps will direct you through installing the roles necessary for starting your first simple RDS server:

1. Open up **Server Manager** and click on the **Add roles and features** link.
2. Click **Next**, which will bring you to the **Installation Type** screen. This is where we differ from normal as far as role installations go. For the majority of roles, we tend to blow right through this screen without a second thought. For Remote Desktop Services, though, we need to make a change on this screen.

3. Choose the option for **Remote Desktop Services installation**. Then click **Next**:

○ **Role-based or feature-based installation**
Configure a single server by adding roles, role services, and features.

◉ **Remote Desktop Services installation**
Install required role services for Virtual Desktop Infrastructure (VDI) to create a virtual machine-based or session-based desktop deployment.

---

4. Leave the default setting as **Standard deployment** and click **Next**. On this screen, we could choose the Quick Start option since we are intending to only configure a single server at this time. I am choosing not to take this shortcut route because we want a good look at the different services that are going to be installed, and want to leave our installation open to having multiple RDS servers down the road.

5. With this RDS server, we are planning to provide access to traditional desktop sessions, not integration with Hyper-V. So, on the **Deployment Scenario** screen, choose **Session-based desktop deployment**:

Remote Desktop Services can be configured to allow users to connect to virtual desktops, RemoteApp programs, and session-based desktops.

○ Virtual machine-based desktop deployment

Virtual machine-based desktop deployment allows users to connect to virtual desktop collections that include published RemoteApp programs and virtual desktops.

◉ Session-based desktop deployment

Session-based desktop deployment allows users to connect to session collections that include published RemoteApp programs and session-based desktops.

---

6. We now see a summary of the role services required for our installation. Based on the options we have chosen, you should see **RD Connection Broker, RD Web Access, and RD Session Host** in this list. The next few screens will be used to define which servers are going to be used for these roles.

7. Since we are installing everything onto a single server, for now, we only have one option in the **Server Pool** list and we simply move it over to the right column. Go ahead and click the arrow to do this on the **RD Connection Broker** page:

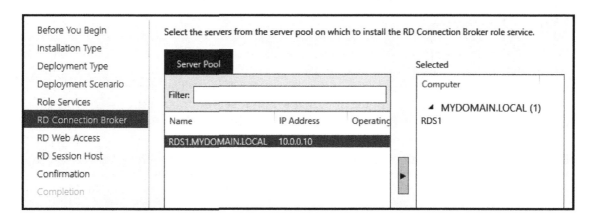

8. Now do the same thing on the next two screens. In our example, we are using the server named RDS1, so I am going to use it as both the RD Web Access server as well as the RD Session Host server.

9. Now you should be up to the **Confirmation** screen, which gives you a summary of the actions about to be performed. For us, all three RDS services are being installed onto the RDS1 server. We must now check the box that says **Restart the destination server automatically if required** and then press the **Deploy** button:

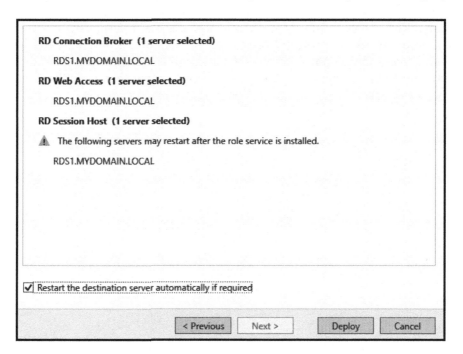

How it works...

We can follow this recipe to get our first simple RDS environment up-and-running. Our server will now allow users to connect and access virtual sessions that are hosted right on this RDS1 server. To log in, users may either launch the Remote Desktop Connection tool on their client computer and type in the RDS1 name of our server or open up a web browser and head over to https://rds1/rdweb. Either way, they will land inside a desktop session that looks and feels pretty similar to a Windows 10 desktop. Inside this desktop provided by the RDS server, they are able to launch applications and save documents, having everything run and stored right on the server itself rather than their local desktop computers. From this simple, single server RDS implementation, we can build and grow out to provide additional RDS roles on more servers, or for the purposes of handling additional user loads.

Adding an additional RDSH server to your RDS environment

Most RDS implementations start out with a single server or at least a single RDSH. Once you have the roles established for successful connectivity here, it is a natural next step to add additional RDSH servers to accommodate more users. Or perhaps you want to segregate different types of users (and their applications) onto different RDSH servers. Whatever your reasoning, chances are that at some point you will want to add additional servers into your RDS environment. Let's add a second server to ours so that you can see how this process works.

Getting ready

We have a single RDS server online, running Windows Server 2016. It is named RDS1 and is already performing the roles of RD Connection Broker, RD Session Host, and RD Web Access. We will now use the management interface on RDS1 in order to add a second RDSH server to our infrastructure. The name of our new server is RDS2, and it is already joined to our domain.

How to do it...

Follow these steps to add a new RDSH server to our existing RDS environment:

1. On the existing RDS server, RDS1, open up **Server Manager**.

 We have to add our new RDS2 server to the instance of Server Manager that is running on RDS1. Until we perform this step, we will be unable to make modifications to RDS2 from here.

2. Click on the **Add other servers to manage** link:

> 2 Add roles and features
>
> 3 Add other servers to manage
>
> 4 Create a server group

3. Type in the name of the new server that you intend to turn into an RDSH. For our example, the server name is RDS2. Then click the arrow to add this server into the **Selected** list and click on **OK**.

4. Now back on the main page of Server Manager, go ahead and click on the listing for **Remote Desktop Services** in the left window pane. This will bring us into the management interface for RDS. Take a look at the **DEPLOYMENT OVERVIEW**, which is a self-generated diagram of what your current RDS deployment looks like. Since we are only testing with our current servers and not accessing them from outside the network, we see plus symbols next to **RD Gateway** and **RD Licensing**. This simply means we have not yet configured these roles, and we could click on those pluses and follow the prompts if we intended to do so. We have no requirement for these services at the present time, so we will ignore this for now:

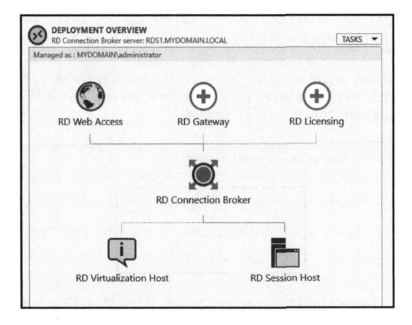

5. To add a new RDSH server, head over to the top right of this window and click on the link that says **Add RD Session Host servers**:

6. Since we added it into Server Manager earlier in the recipe, we should now be able to see in this list the new server available to select. Select the new RDS2 server and click the arrow to move it into the **Selected** column. Then click **Add**:

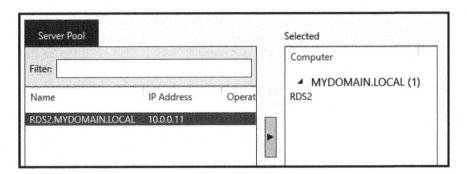

7. Click the **Next** button, and you will need to check the box that says **Restart remote computers as needed** on the **Confirmation** screen. Then click on **Add**:

How it works...

In this recipe, we used the Remote Desktop Services management console on our primary RDS server to take a new server that we had running and turn it into a **Remote Desktop Session Host (RDSH)** server. This RDSH is now part of our RDS infrastructure, and can be managed right from this centralized management platform. In an RDS environment, this is typically the way that new roles are added onto servers that are being brought into the environment. Using the centralized management console to perform many tasks in RDS makes a lot of sense, because it is easy to see the big picture of your RDS infrastructure as you make changes or updates.

Installing applications on a Remote Desktop Session Host server

As soon as you take a Windows Server and turn it into a RDSH server to be used within an RDS environment, the way that applications work on that server changes significantly. Whenever programs and apps are installed onto that RDSH, it first needs to be put into a special *Install Mode*. Placing the server into Install Mode prior to launching the program installer is important to make sure that applications are going to be installed in a way that will allow multiple users to run them simultaneously. Remember, our RDSH servers will be hosting multiple user sessions, probably dozens of them.

Using Install Mode is so important to applications working properly on an RDSH that you really should not install any programs onto the server before you turn it into an RDSH. Once that role has been established, then apps can be safely installed, as long as you are using Install Mode. Programs installed prior to converting that server into an RDSH may not work properly, and you might have to uninstall and reinstall them. There are a couple of different ways that Install Mode can be invoked during a program installation; let's take a look at both of them.

Getting ready

We need to install a program onto our RDSH server. This box is running Windows Server 2016 and is already part of our RDS environment. We will also need, of course, the application installer files that we intend to launch.

How to do it...

One way to properly install programs onto an RDSH is by using Control Panel to install the application:

1. Right-click on your **Start** flag and choose to open Control Panel
2. Click on **Programs**
3. Choose the button that says **Install Application on Remote Desktop...**:

4. Click **Next** and you will be able to specify the location of your installer file for the application:

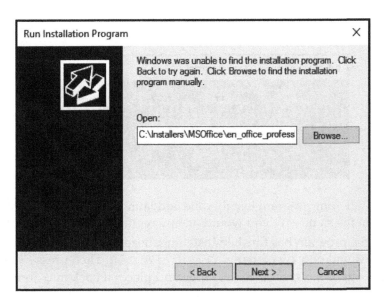

5. Click **Next**, and your program will install. When finished, make sure you click the **Finish** button on the Install Mode mini-wizard screen, so that the RDSH is placed back into Execute Mode and is ready for normal operation:

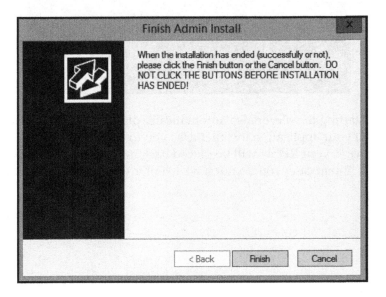

The second way to place an RDSH into Install Mode is by using the command prompt:

1. Right-click on the **Start** flag and choose to open **Command Prompt (Admin)**.
2. Type change user /install and press *Enter*:

```
Administrator: Command Prompt

C:\>change user /install
User session is ready to install applications.

C:\>
```

3. Now find your program installer file and launch it. Walk through the installation steps in the same way you would on any regular server or computer.
4. Once the program has finished installing, head back to the command prompt window and now type change user /execute. Then press *Enter*. This takes the RDSH out of the special Install Mode and places it back into normal Execute Mode:

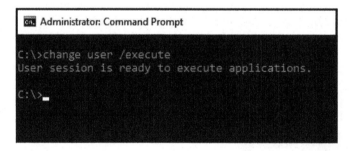

```
Administrator: Command Prompt

C:\>change user /execute
User session is ready to execute applications.

C:\>
```

Restarting the server also automatically places it back into Execute Mode. So if your application installer asks you to restart as part of the installation process, your RDSH will be placed back into Execute Mode when it boots, and in that case, you do not have to enter the command manually.

How it works...

When installing applications onto an RDSH, it must first be placed into a special Install Mode. Doing this re-maps certain parts of the program being installed so that it can be run and utilized by many users at the same time. Installing your applications by using one of the methods discussed in this recipe will be critical to the success of your RDS environment being able to provide applications to users.

Also keep in mind that it is recommended you have no users logged into an RDSH during the time of installation. When you are building fresh servers, this is easy as you don't typically allow anyone to connect until everything is installed and configured. But if you need to install new programs or updates to existing programs onto a production RDSH, you will want to take steps to ensure that users are not logged in to the server before you place it into Install Mode and launch those executables. If you are running a farm of RDS servers and want to remove just one or some of them for maintenance or the installation of an application, make sure to check out the *Removing an RD Session Host server from use for maintenance* recipe.

I mentioned placing the RDSH into Install Mode even when just installing updates to existing applications. This is important. However, you do not need to place a server into Install Mode in order to install regular Windows operating system updates. These are able to install correctly even when the server is in normal Execute Mode.

Disabling the redirection of local resources

One of the neat things about users connecting to virtual sessions within an RDS environment, especially when connecting remotely, is local resource redirection. This feature enables the users to have access to things that are local to where they are sitting, from inside their virtual session, such as the clipboard, so that copy and paste functions will work between local computer and RDS session and drive redirection so that you can save documents back and forth between the local hard drive and the RDS session. One of the most common uses of resource redirection is printers so that users can print from inside their RDS session, which is sitting on a server in the corporate network, directly to a printer on the local network where they are connected. An example could be someone needing to print a work document on a home printer.

This redirection technology can be very helpful but is often not desirable from a security and policies standpoint. Many organizations have a written security policy, which dictates that corporate data must remain within the corporate network and cannot move outside. Most often I see this in medical environments, where strict standards are in place to make sure data stays private and secure. This means that data cannot be copied and pasted to the local computer, documents cannot be saved outside the RDS session, and printing documents is also often not allowed.

While it may be disappointing that you cannot use these functions if your security policy dictates it, thankfully disabling redirection is an easy thing to accomplish. Follow along to learn where these settings reside.

Getting ready

We are logged into our Server 2016 RDSH server. This server is hosting some sensitive information and we want to make sure that users cannot save documents to their local computers, cannot print documents to local printers, and cannot copy/paste within the clipboard in order to move data from the RDS session to their local computers.

How to do it...

Follow along to disable these redirection features on our RDSH collection:

1. Open up **Server Manager** and click on **Remote Desktop Services** to open up the management of your RDS environment.
2. We currently only have one RDSH collection listed, which contains both of our RDSH servers. This is the collection that all of our users connect to when they have to access this sensitive information. Click on the name of that collection. For our example, this one is called **MDomain RDSH Servers**.
3. Near the top of the screen, look for the section called **Properties**. Drop down the **Tasks** box and click on **Edit Properties**:

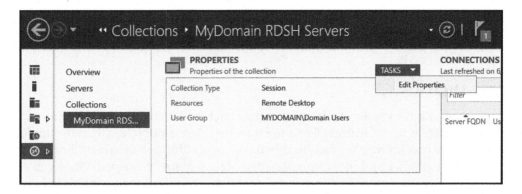

4. Click on **Client Settings**.
5. Here is your list of the items that are currently capable of being redirected. Go ahead and deselect each of the redirections that you want to disable. For our example, we are unchecking **Drives**, **Clipboard**, and **Allow client printer redirection**:

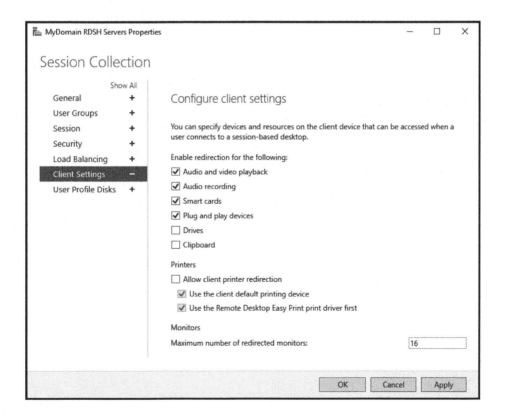

6. Click **OK** and those redirected resources are no longer available to client computers connecting to this RDSH collection.

How it works...

Providing users with the capability of moving data back and forth between their local computers and RDS sessions sounds like a great feature, but is often less than desirable. With some simple checkboxes, we can disable these capabilities wholesale so that you can adhere to security policies and make sure sensitive data remains protected. Once you are familiar with the location of these settings, the enablement or disablement of them is intuitive and easy to accomplish. What is even better is that these settings can be changed at any time; it doesn't have to be a decision made while the RDS environment is being built. If you make the decision down the road to turn some of these options on or off, you can make these changes at any time to a production RDS.

Shadowing another session in RDS

Let's say you receive a phone call from a remote user in your company; they are currently sitting in a hotel and are having trouble figuring out how to open an application. This application isn't installed on their local computer, they are an RDS user, and they connect into a virtual session on an RDSH server in your network whenever they need to access this app. You think about asking for their password, as that way you could just log into the RDSH as them and take care of the problem. But alas, asking for a password is a serious breach of company security policy. Instead, perhaps you can use some kind of online meeting software to share the screen of their laptop and try to walk them through fixing the problem. But that would mean walking them through the installation of that meeting software and hoping you could explain over the phone how to use it.

Looking for a better solution? Use the *Shadowing* feature of RDS. If you log in to the RDSH server where the user is already logged in, you can simply shadow their session in order to see what they are seeing. You can then work together to resolve the issue. You'll be able to take control and fix the problem, and maybe they can even take some notes and learn how to do it themselves next time to save the phone call.

This recipe is included here particularly because RDS Shadowing was always available in older versions of Terminal Server, but was then removed from Server 2012 RDS. Well, good news! It was brought back by popular demand in Server 2012 R2, and remains here to stay in Windows Server 2016!

Getting ready

Our remote user is logged into a virtual session on our RDSH server, which is called RDS1. This is a Server 2016 machine that is part of our RDS infrastructure.

How to do it...

Let's help out this remote user by shadowing their RD session:

1. First, we need to log into the same RDSH server that the user is logged into. On your computer, open **Remote Desktop Connection** and input the server name in order to connect.

2. Now that you are logged into the RDSH, right-click on the Taskbar and open **Task Manager**:

3. Click on **More details** in order to see more information about the server.

4. Navigate to the **Users** tab.

5. Right-click on one of the column headings and choose to show the **ID** column:

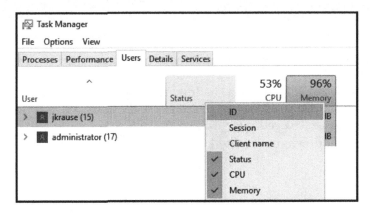

6. Leave Task Manager open so that you can see the username that you want to connect to and their ID number.

7. Now open a Command Prompt and type the following: `mstsc /shadow:<id> /control`. So for our particular **jkrause** user, who is currently running on ID 3 as you can see inside Task Manager, we use this command: `mstsc /shadow:3 /control`:

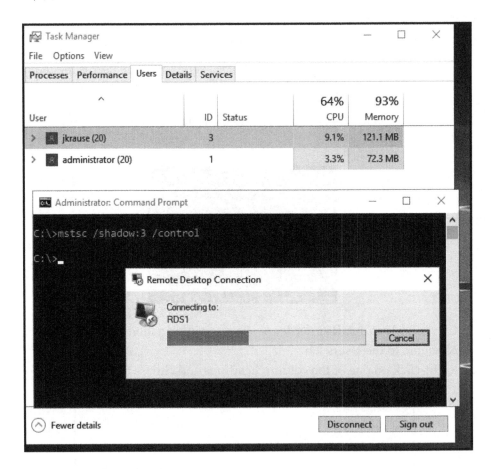

8. This command will launch a shadowing session to the RD session of the ID number that you used, so make sure to use the correct ID for the user you want to shadow. Since we used the `/control` switch, you should also have the capability of using your own mouse and keyboard inside the user's session.

How it works...

While shadowing in Server 2016 isn't quite as easy as it used to be in earlier versions of Terminal Server, it's great to know that this capability has returned after a noticeable absence in Server 2012. RDS Shadowing is a great tool to use for troubleshooting or collaboration, as it enables you to share the screen of other personnel and assist with your own keyboard and mouse control when necessary. Having two sets of eyes on the same RD session can be invaluable in many situations; go try it out today!

Installing a printer driver to use with redirection

When a user connects to an RD session, if the client and server are configured properly, that connection will attempt to set up printer redirection between the RD session and the local computer. Specifically, what happens is that every printer that is installed onto the local computer will be configured as a separate printer inside the user's RD session. This is the feature that enables users to be able to print to their local printers, even if the information that they are accessing and printing is located halfway around the world.

When the RD connection builds these virtual printers, it attempts to use real printer drivers for them. For example, if the printer is an HP LaserJet 4100 and the RDSH server has the HP LaserJet 4100 driver installed, then when that printer gets set up inside the user session, it will utilize that existing, official driver. If the user logs into an RDSH with a printer whose driver does not exist on the RDSH server, however, by default that printer will not be installed. There is a setting in the same configuration page where we enable or disable printer redirection on the RDSH server collection that can partially help with this. If you select the option on that screen for **Use the Remote Desktop Easy Print print driver first**, when the real driver doesn't exist for a particular printer, it will use a generic driver that may or may not actually work with the printer. This can certainly help bridge the gap when it comes to missing printer drivers but doesn't always solve the problem.

The best way to make sure your users are going to be able to print properly is to install the real driver onto the RDSH. So what's the point of this recipe? Who doesn't know how to install a printer driver, right? I write this because most printer driver software packages are now full-blown applications, and we don't need a quarter of what comes with them. Driver install packages consume much more space than necessary for use with RDS, and we have to take into consideration that we are installing actual applications, which could potentially show up inside user sessions and cause confusion. So what is the answer? Extract the simple driver files from those driver packages and use just the files themselves in order to install the driver into Windows. Let's do one together so you can see what I'm talking about.

Getting ready

We will be installing this printer driver onto our RDSH server running Windows Server 2016. For our example, we will be using a Brother MFC-J625DW printer, since that is one I installed for a customer just recently. Brother is usually good about providing a simple, small driver download that contains only the files we need for the driver itself.

How to do it...

Let's work together to download and install this printer driver onto our RDSH so that it can be used for printer redirection:

1. First, download the driver files onto your RDSH server. Make sure to choose the driver for the server's operating system, not the client. So when possible, I am going to choose Windows Server 2016. You can see in the following list that Windows Server 2016 is not an option available to me with this particular model of printer, and that is okay. In the event that the actual operating system driver is not available, you can often use one from a recent version of Windows and make it work. I will attempt to download the Windows 10 64-bit driver and see if it will install onto my Windows Server 2016. Alternatively, I could probably also get the Windows Server 2012 R2 64-bit driver to install as well:

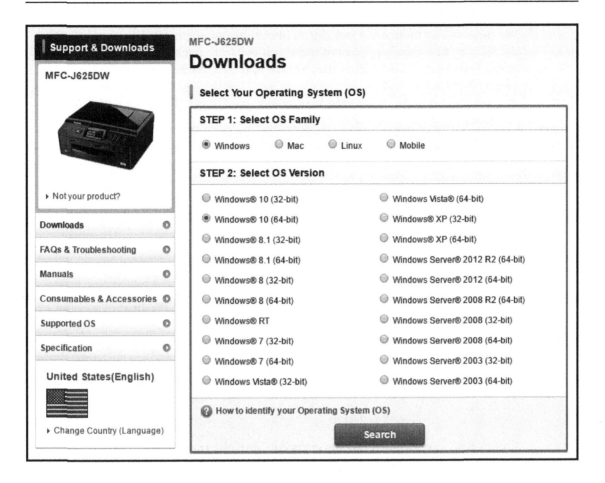

2. We can see that there are a few different options available for downloading the driver. The first that is presented is the full software package, but that is 134 MB and remember we said earlier that the full software package is totally unnecessary on an RDS server. We only need the driver. A little further down the page, there is an option for **Add Printer Wizard Driver**. This is exactly what we need, and what do you know, it's only 23 MB!:

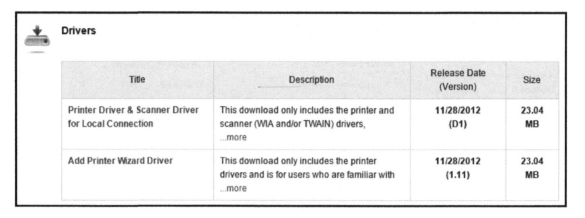

Drivers

Title	Description	Release Date (Version)	Size
Printer Driver & Scanner Driver for Local Connection	This download only includes the printer and scanner (WIA and/or TWAIN) drivers, ...more	11/28/2012 (D1)	23.04 MB
Add Printer Wizard Driver	This download only includes the printer drivers and is for users who are familiar with ...more	11/28/2012 (1.11)	23.04 MB

With most driver downloads, you will also have to double-click on it once downloaded in order to extract the files.

3. Right-click on your **Start** flag and choose **Control Panel**.
4. Navigate to **Hardware | View devices and printers**.
5. Click on any existing printer in the list and then click on the button in the top Taskbar that says **Print server properties**:

Devices and Printers

← → ˅ ↑ 🖶 › Control Panel › Hardware › Devices and Printers ˅ ↻

Add a device   Add a printer   See what's printing   Print server properties   Remove device

6. Browse to the **Drivers** tab. This displays a list of currently installed printer drivers on this server. Then click the **Add...** button.

7. Click **Next** twice. We can leave the **Processor Selection** screen marked as only **x64**, since Windows Server 2016 only comes in 64-bit.

8. Now click on **Have Disk...** and browse to the location of the driver files that you downloaded. You are looking for an INF file that typically sits in the root of that driver folder. Sometimes you will have to poke around a little until you find it, but the file is always an INF file:

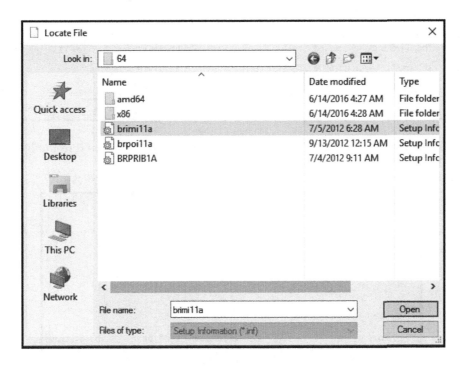

9. Once you have selected the INF file, the **Add Printer Driver Wizard** will now display a list of the drivers that are contained within that INF file. Choose the specific printer driver that you want to install and click **Next**:

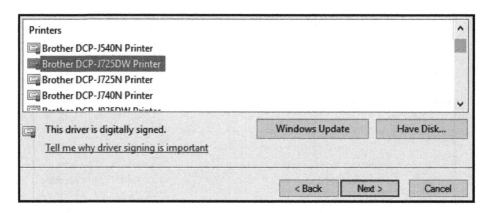

10. Click **Finish** and the driver will install. You should now see it in the list of printer drivers that are installed on this server:

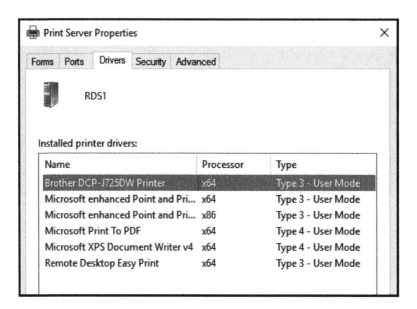

How it works...

Installing printer drivers onto RDSH servers is a pretty common administrative task in environments where printer redirection is allowed. We walked through one of the nice, simple installers that was easy to extract and contained only the actual driver files that we needed. These kinds of driver downloads are perfect for our purposes here.

As you experience more and more of these driver installations, you will start to learn which manufacturers provide simple driver packages for this purpose and which ones do not. Ultimately, though, the software always contains the simple driver files; sometimes it's just a matter of launching the huge installer program so that it places the files somewhere in a temporary location on the hard drive. What I normally do in these situations is launch the installer and walk it through whatever steps are necessary in order to see that it is unpacking/extracting files. Once it has done that, you don't have to run any more of the wizard to install the software applications because you know that the driver files you need are sitting on the hard drive of the server somewhere. We just need to find them. Using a utility such as FileMon can help identify file locations that have been recently modified, and is a pretty quick way to track down those driver files that are usually hidden away in a `temp` folder. Once you find the files, you can copy and paste them into a more permanent folder for driver installation purposes, cancel out of the install wizard, and walk through the steps in this recipe to install that driver manually instead.

Removing an RD Session Host server from use for maintenance

Occasionally, you will have to perform some maintenance on your RDSH servers. Whether it is for installing updates, installing new applications, or taking them down for some physical maintenance, it will happen sooner or later. If you have multiple RDSH servers in a collection and simply take one offline, user loads will eventually sort themselves out as the RD broker will send new connections to the RDSH servers that are still online, but you will have caused frustration and headaches for any users who were logged in when you shut it down. It is much more user-friendly to flag an RDSH to make it unable to accept new user connections and let the existing ones dissolve naturally over a period of time. This is kind of like a *drain stop* in the NLB world.

Let's take a look at the setting included in RDS that allows us to flag an RDSH as unusable and force the broker to keep new connections from coming through to it. We'll also reverse that change to make sure it starts accepting user connections again after our maintenance is complete.

Getting ready

We have an RDS environment configured with two RDSH servers. These are called RDS1 and RDS2, and we are required to do some maintenance on RDS2. All of our work will be accomplished from inside the Remote Desktop management console on RDS1.

How to do it...

To stop new user connections from flowing to RDS2:

1. Open **Server Manager** and click on **Remote Desktop Services** in the left window pane.
2. Navigate to **Collections** | **MyDomain RDSH Servers**. This is the name of the collection in my environment; you will need to click on whatever the name of your collection is.
3. Scroll down to the bottom, where you can see the **Host Servers** section. This is a list of the RDSH servers that are part of your collection.
4. Right-click on the RDSH server that we need to perform some maintenance on. In our case, it is **RDS2**.
5. Click on **Do not allow new connections**:

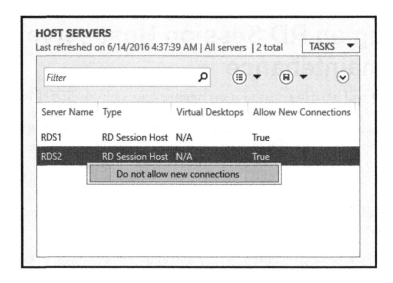

6. This will cause any new connections to be sent over to RDS1 or whatever other RDSH servers you have in your collection. Then, once your maintenance is complete and you are ready to reintroduce RDS2 back into the collection, simply right-click on its name here again and this time choose **Allow new connections**:

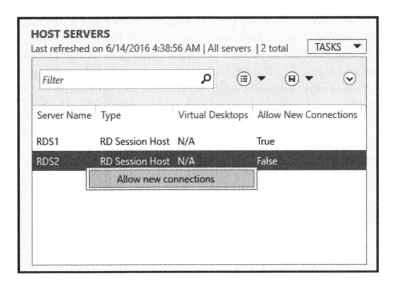

How it works...

This simple option can be a very helpful utility when considering maintenance within your RDS infrastructure. Remember, disallowing new connections to a particular RDSH does not mean that it is immediately available for maintenance because existing users will still be logged in to it. We have only set it so that no new connections will flow there. You can give it some planned time to naturally drop the remaining connections that do exist on the server before performing your maintenance.

Publishing WordPad with RemoteApp

Most of the recipes in this chapter are focused on full desktop sessions provided by RDSH servers because this is the most common scenario that I find RDS used for in the field. One additional piece I would like to take a quick look into is RemoteApp publishing. This is the ability to publish individual applications out to remote users from an RDSH server, rather than a full desktop session. It provides a seamless window for the application, allowing the RemoteApp to look and feel like any other program on the user's computer. Let's set up a sample application and test using it from a client computer. For the sake of simplicity in demonstrating this capability, we will use WordPad as our application to publish and launch.

Getting ready

Our work to publish WordPad as a RemoteApp will be performed from our Server 2016 RDSH called RDS1. We will also use a client computer in order to test accessing this application once we are finished publishing it.

How to do it...

To publish WordPad as a RemoteApp, follow these steps:

1. On RDS1, launch **Server Manager** and click on **Remote Desktop Services** from the left window pane.
2. Browse to the collection of RDSH servers where you want to publish this new application. For our example, I am browsing to **Collections | MyDomain RDSH Servers.**
3. Near the middle of this window, you will see a section called **REMOTEAPP PROGRAMS**. Click on the link in the middle of this window that says **Publish RemoteApp programs**:

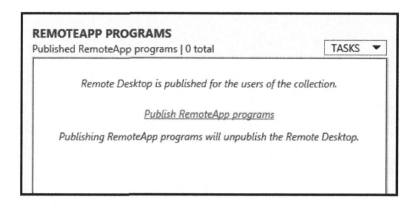

4. The wizard will now poll the server for a list of available applications. Look through the list until you see **WordPad**; it is most likely on the bottom. Choose it and click **Next**:

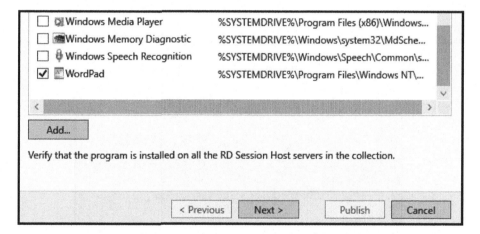

5. On the **Confirmation** screen, click **Publish**.
6. Now that we have the WordPad application published, log in to a client computer so that we can test accessing it.

7. On the client computer, open up a web browser and navigate to
   `https://RDS1/RDweb`:

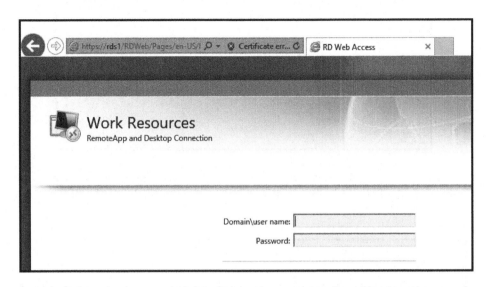

8. Input your credentials, and you should see our published resources that are available in the RDS environment. As expected, WordPad is now visible here:

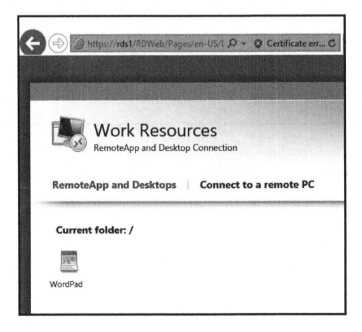

9. Click on the **WordPad** icon and it opens on your computer:

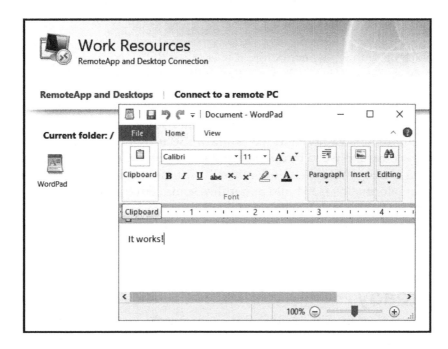

How it works...

If you do not have a need for users to receive access to a full desktop when they log in to the RDS environment, you have the option of publishing individual applications instead. This can be useful for restricting the resources that employees have access to, or perhaps for someone such as a vendor or a temporary assignment that only needs access to certain programs and data. While this was a very simple demonstration using the WordPad program baked into Windows, you can use this same process with other applications you have installed onto your RDSH servers yourself.

Make sure you install the applications onto all of the RDSH servers in your collection.

Tracking user logins with Logon/Logoff scripts

I have been working with RDS since before it was called RDS, and something that absolutely every single customer asks for is the ability to report on which users are connecting to which RDSH servers. Ideally, they would like to be able to see, historically, a list of people logging in, and sometimes even some data about when the user logged off the server as well. The only information I have ever found natively inside Windows that can help with this information gathering is the Windows Security Event Logs, but those are extremely messy to try and weed through to find what you are looking for. It's definitely not worth the hassle. So what's the solution here? The easiest way I have found to record login and logout information is to build and utilize some scripts that will run during every user logon and logoff. This is quite simple to do on each of your RDSH servers; let's give it a try together so you can have an idea of what I typically do, and then you can adjust from there based on your specific needs.

Getting ready

Here, we are going to build a couple of scripts on our RDS1 server, which is a Remote Desktop Session Host. Everything we will do is right on this Windows Server 2016 box.

How to do it...

Follow these steps to start recording information about user logins on your RDSH servers:

1. Log into RDS1 and create a new batch file. We are going to utilize good old batch file scripts, but you could also create something with PowerShell to accomplish the same function. I find, however, that a single line of code inside a batch file does the trick quite well. I have created the following script on mine:
   `C:\Reporting\Logon.bat`

2. Now right-click on that script, and choose **Edit** in order to open it up in Notepad.

3. Input the following text:

```
Echo %date%,%time%,%username%,%computername% >>
C:\Reporting\Logons.txt
```

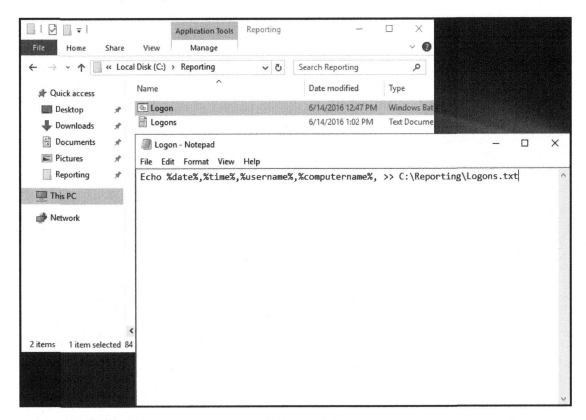

4. Now you need to copy your logon script and place it inside the following folder: C:\Windows\System32\grouppolicy\user\scripts\logon.

You may have to create this folder structure if it doesn't already exist.

5. Now open up `gpedit.msc` and navigate to `User Configuration | Windows Settings | Scripts (Logon/Logoff)`. Go ahead and specify your **Logon** script here:

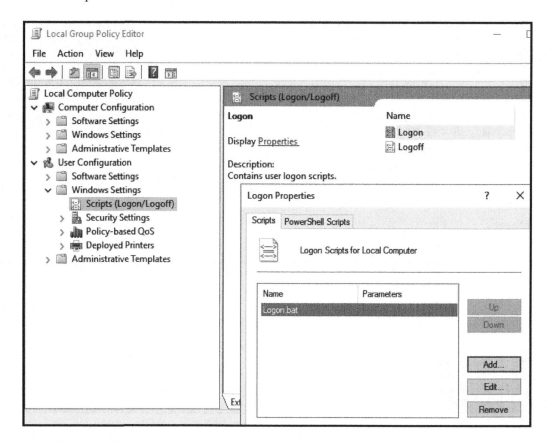

6. With this single command, we are logging quite a bit of data into the Logons.txt file: the current date, time, user's login name, and the RDSH server name they are logging into. Go ahead and log in to RDS1 a few times with different user accounts, and then open up this text file. You can see some information now being logged:

```
Logons - Notepad
File   Edit   Format   View   Help
Tue 06/14/2016,12:54:37.46,administrator,RDS1
Tue 06/14/2016,12:55:00.79,jkrause,RDS1
Tue 06/14/2016,12:57:50.45,administrator,RDS1
Tue 06/14/2016,12:57:54.31,jkrause,RDS1
```

 I typically use commas to separate the pieces of data so that this text file can be imported into Excel later to be further manipulated and categorized.

Alternatively, you could utilize two separate batch files, one for logons, and one for logoffs. I like this method because we can also split up the logging into multiple smaller text files, one for each username. Then we can see very quickly all the times that each username logged in and logged out. Here is an example of how to accomplish that:

1. **Logon script:** `Echo LOGON,%date%,%time%,%username%,%computername% >> "C:\Reporting\%username%.log"`.

2. **Logoff script:** `Echo LOGOFF,%date%,%time%,%username%,%computername% >> "C:\Reporting\%username%.log"`.

3. Place your new Logon script inside `C:\Windows\System32\grouppolicy\user\scripts\logon`.

4. Place your new Logoff script inside `C:\Windows\System32\grouppolicy\user\scripts\logoff`.

5. Inside `gpedit.msc`, make sure that you incorporate both the **Logon** and **Logoff** scripts. These are in the same location we visited before.

6. Once your logon and logoff scripts are copied into the right places and specified inside gpedit, you can start logging in and out of your RDS1 server. After a few attempts, take a look inside the `C:\Reporting` folder. Now we have multiple text files listed here, one for each username. Inside each text file we can see timestamps for both logons and logoffs that were performed by that user. It's pretty neat data collection for how simple those scripts are!

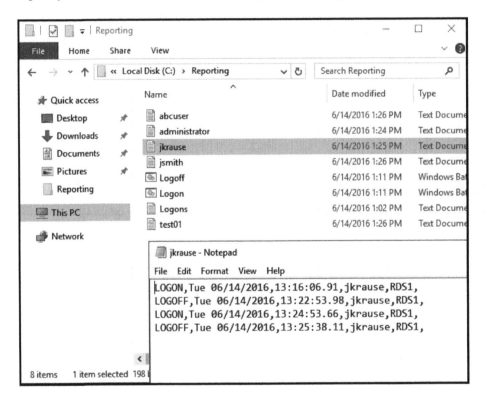

How it works...

We can utilize some very simple logon and logoff scripts on RDSH servers in order to generate reporting information about who is logging in, where they are logging in, and at what times they are coming and leaving. Incorporating these reporting scripts onto each of your RDSH servers and then having them all report to a central location can greatly improve your ability to generate user accounting information. This is a common question among those utilizing RDS, and hopefully you can take this information and build on top of it further to gather whatever info is important to your organization.

5
Monitoring and Backup

Monitoring and backing up servers are usually mundane tasks that are easily overlooked or forgotten. When everything is running smoothly, you may not even think about whether or not your servers have backed up properly, maybe for weeks at a time. Except in the largest of companies, there usually aren't dedicated backup admins or performance monitoring gurus. In IT, we all wear many different hats, and they don't always fit on top of each other.

The key phrase above is *when everything is running smoothly*. Unfortunately, this state of bliss cannot continue indefinitely. Hardware fails, malware happens, files are accidentally deleted. Suddenly, those dull chores of due diligence, such as monitoring the health of your servers and making sure you have solid backups, jumps from backburner to mission-critical on the importance scale.

The good news is that monitoring and backups have never been easier than they are in Windows Server 2016. Let's explore together some of the tools that exist to make these areas of your infrastructure efficient and automatic:

- Using Server Manager as a quick monitoring tool
- Using the new Task Manager to its full potential
- Evaluating system performance with Windows Performance Monitor
- Using Format-List to modify PowerShell data output
- Configuring a full system backup using Windows Server Backup
- Recovering data from a Windows backup file
- Using IP Address Management to keep track of your used IP addresses
- Checking for viruses in Windows Server 2016

Introduction

There are many third-party tools available for performing functions such as data backups and performance monitoring, and because these tools exist, it is easy to automatically assume that they will do a better job than anything that comes with the operating system. Given that, we often categorize backups and monitoring into areas where we will have to spend extra money. I'm not trying to argue that every add-on tool for these functions is unnecessary because they do certainly benefit the right kinds of company. But anyone willing to dig into Server 2016 and discover what it can accomplish on its own accord, without extra add-ons, I think you will find that it meets the needs of many businesses.

Using Server Manager as a quick monitoring tool

Sometimes change is difficult for us old-school IT guys. You know, the ones who prefer keyboards over mice and command lines over graphical interfaces. Starting in Server 2012, Server Manager changed a lot. I find that many admins automatically dislike it, even before they have started using it. It looks *cloudy*, full of links to click on rather than applications. It's certainly more of a web app interface than the Server Manager we are used to.

Let's use this recipe to point out some of the important data that exists in Server Manager, and discover for ourselves that Microsoft may actually have a valid point in causing it to open automatically every time that you log in to a server. No, it's not just there to annoy you.

Getting ready

All we need is Windows Server 2016 in order to poke around in Server Manager. The server we are using is domain joined with a few roles installed so that we can get a better feel for the layout of data on a production system.

How to do it...

Follow these steps to discover some of the functions that Server Manager can perform:

1. Open up **Server Manager**. If you just logged into your server, it is probably opening automatically. Otherwise, click on the **Server Manager** button inside your Start menu.

2. Normally, at the top of Server Manager is the section entitled **Welcome to Server Manager**. In the lower right corner of that section is a button that says **Hide**. Go ahead and click on that button to hide this section of the screen.

3. Now take a look at the information on your screen. These normally green bars listed under each service that you have installed are your first indication as to whether or not everything is running smoothly. Everything is green on mine, which indicates that everything is working properly:

4. Now I'm going to break my AD DS service purposefully to demonstrate what it looks like when things aren't running smoothly. You may or may not want to do this depending on whether or not you are looking at this on a production server. I have stopped my DFSR service on this box, and now see the following in Server Manager:

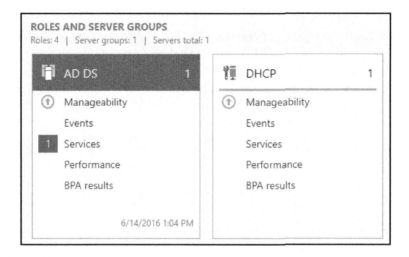

5. If I click on the **Services** button, where it is indicating that I have one notification, I can see the details of what is going on. Right from here I have the ability to right-click on the warning message and choose a repair method of **Start Services**:

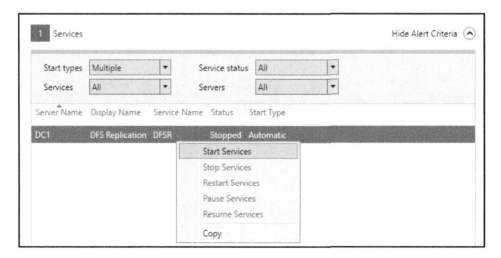

6. There is a button near the bottom of this screen that says **Go To AD DS**. Go ahead and click on that button and you will see that it brings us to the same screen as if we had clicked on **AD DS** in the left window pane in Server Manager. On this screen, we can see even more information about our AD DS role and any trouble that it may be having:

 For any role that you have installed on your server, there is a quick link to that role's section of Server Manager in the left window pane. Click on each role to view events and information specific to that role.

7. Now click on **Local Server** from the left window pane. Here we see a number of items listed that are helpful for troubleshooting any facet of the operating system, and for reviewing the general status and health of the server. Scroll down near the bottom of this page for a list of events that are happening on this server, without having to open a separate **Events** window:

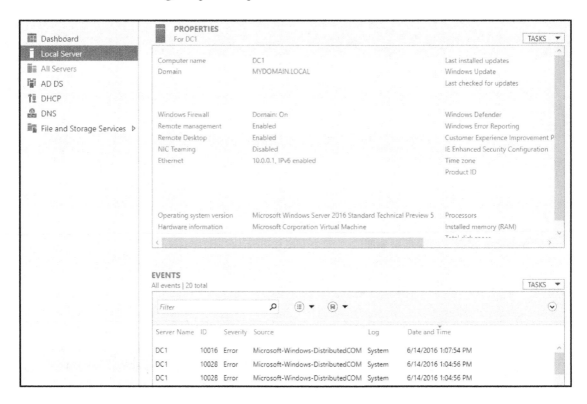

8. Many of the items listed inside this **Local Server** screen are links to open additional configuration windows. For example, where it tells us that **the IE Enhanced Security Configuration** is currently **On**, if we click on **On**, we get the properties page for configuring the IE Enhanced Security Configuration settings on this server:

How it works...

Server Manager is full of opportunities to quickly find information that will help monitor your servers. This recipe is just a sample of the data that you can pull into Server Manager, so I suggest you continue navigating around in there to make it look and feel the best that it can for your environment. Another extremely helpful option here is to add multiple servers into your Server Manager for monitoring purposes. If you use the **Manage** menu near the top and the **Add Servers** function in that menu, you can add additional systems into your Server Manager window pane. Doing this causes Server Manager to pull information not only about the local server that you are logged in to, but also about these remote servers, all into one pane of glass. This way you can use Server Manager on one server in order to monitor and maintain your entire server infrastructure if you choose to do so.

Using the new Task Manager to its full potential

We have all used *Ctrl + Alt + Delete* to open Task Manager and attempt to close problematic applications. With the Task Manager provided by Windows Server 2016, we can do much more right from that same interface. Let's work through this recipe to explore some of the new things that can be done to take full advantage of this tool.

Getting ready

We are logged into a Windows Server 2016 server. This is the only system required for our recipe.

How to do it...

Follow these steps to learn a little more about Task Manager:

1. Right-click on the Taskbar and choose to open **Task Manager**. This is an alternate way to get into the utility, other than using the *Ctrl + Alt + Delete* key combination. I prefer using the Taskbar right-click in fact because, when using the keyboard, it is easy to open the wrong Task Manager when you are using a virtualization console or RDP to administer remote servers.

2. You are now looking at the simple version of Task Manager, where you can choose an application and click **End task** in order to forcibly close that application. To dig a little deeper, click on the **More details** link near the bottom:

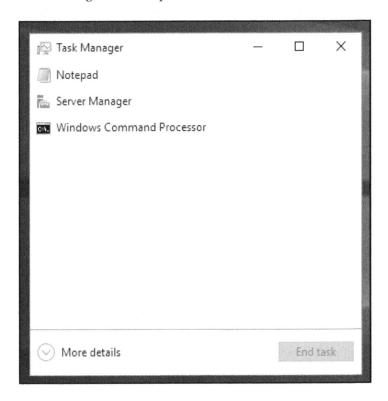

3. Now this is more like it! We can see all open applications at a quick glance, including how many resources each one is consuming. This makes it pretty easy to identify applications that might be stuck and consuming large amounts of CPU or memory. It also lists **Background processes** separately, which can be hugely helpful for finding malware or rogue processes:

Task Manager			
File Options View			
Processes Performance Users Details Services			
		7%	**71%**
Name		CPU	Memory
Apps (4)			
> 　Notepad		0%	1.4 MB
> 　Server Manager		0%	100.7 MB
> 　Task Manager		0%	7.9 MB
> 　Windows Command Processor		0%	0.4 MB
Background processes (18)			
> 　Distributed File System Replicati...		0%	9.3 MB
> 　Domain Name System (DNS) Se...		0%	12.1 MB
Host Process for Windows Tasks		0%	1.1 MB
Host Process for Windows Tasks		0%	2.1 MB
Host process for WinRM plug-ins		0%	55.4 MB
> 　Microsoft Distributed Transacti...		0%	1.4 MB
> 　Microsoft.ActiveDirectory.WebS...		0%	9.3 MB
> 　Microsoft® Volume Shadow Co...		0%	1.8 MB

4. The **Details** and **Services** tabs are pretty self-explanatory. **Details** will show even more information about the individual processes that are running and consuming resources on your server. The **Services** tab shows a list of services installed on your server and their current statuses.

5. Click on the **Users** tab and then click the arrow listed under your username to see the expanded view. Listed under each username are the applications that they have open. This sorted list of running programs is especially nice when logged into a server hosting many user connections at once, such as a Remote Desktop Session Host:

User	Status	3% CPU	69% Memory
⌄ Administrator (17)		2.8%	207.4 MB
Client Server Runtime Proc...		0%	0.9 MB
Console Window Host		0%	4.7 MB
Desktop Window Manager		0%	19.3 MB
Host Process for Windows ...		0%	1.1 MB
Host Process for Windows ...		0%	2.1 MB
Host process for WinRM pl...		0%	55.3 MB
Notepad		0%	1.1 MB
Runtime Broker		0%	2.2 MB
Search		0%	0.1 MB
Server Manager		0%	100.7 MB
Service Host: Unistack Serv...		0%	1.6 MB
Shell Infrastructure Host		0%	2.7 MB
Task Manager		2.8%	7.6 MB
Windows Command Proce...		0%	0.3 MB

6. Now browse over to the **Performance** tab. You will find that this screen looks much nicer than in previous versions. You can click between the different performance counters on the left to see the different details. If you right-click on the graph itself, you will notice there are some additional options. You can click on **Graph summary view** in order to change the Task Manager window into a smaller, graph-only mode that you can leave running in the corner of the screen. You can also choose to copy the screen, which can be helpful for grabbing a quick copy of this data and sending it on for troubleshooting or monitoring purposes:

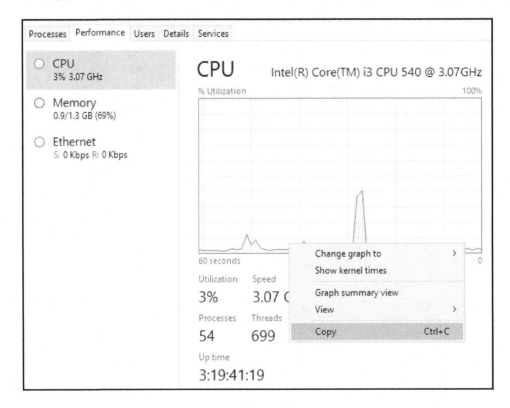

7. At the bottom of your Task Manager screen, click on **Open Resource Monitor**. This runs the new Resource Monitor, which is an even more extensive tool for monitoring hardware resources and utilization. This is very helpful for monitoring hardware in real time:

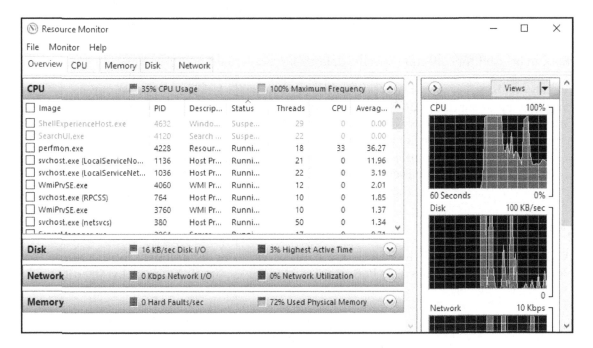

How it works...

The new Task Manager provided with Server 2016 contains many additional pieces of information that are helpful for monitoring system performance in real time. As you start to administer your new Server 2016 machines, make sure you spend some time in this interface so that you are familiar with the new layout when you need to access information quickly.

Evaluating system performance with Windows Performance Monitor

While good old Task Manager and the new Resource Monitor are great utilities for monitoring system performance in real time, for any more extensive monitoring needs I tend to prefer Performance Monitor. Perfmon, as it is often nicknamed, is an excellent tool that can be used for collecting specific data over a predefined period of time.

We have all had cases where a report comes across our desk that a certain server is misbehaving or running slowly. By the time we get logged in, everything looks normal. Other than Event Viewer, we don't have a whole lot of options for investigating what was happening during the time of the problem. But it might happen again, and if we plan ahead with the Performance Monitor tool, we might be able to catch the server in the act, even if we don't see the data until after the event has finished.

Getting ready

We will be monitoring a Windows Server 2016 server in our environment for this recipe. Nothing needs to be installed, as Performance Monitor is part of Windows by default.

How to do it...

In order to collect server performance data using Performance Monitor, follow these steps:

1. Open up a command prompt or your **Run** box and type perfmon. This will launch the Performance Monitor tool:

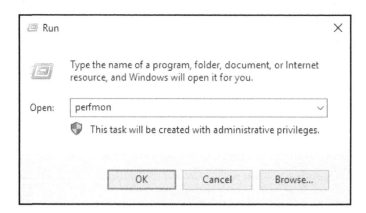

2. From the left window pane, navigate to **Monitoring Tools | Performance Monitor**. You can see that it shows some real-time data about the processor by default:

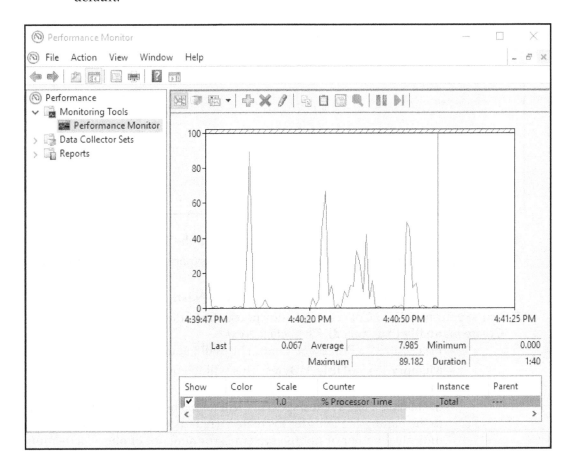

3. Browse to **Data Collector Sets** | **User Defined**. Right-click on this folder and choose **New** | **Data Collector Set**:

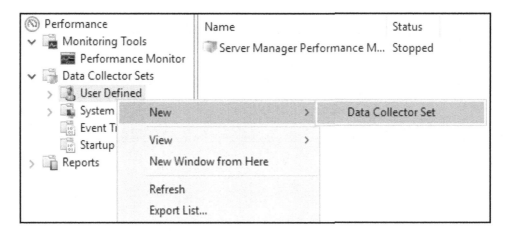

4. For my evaluation on this server, I am going to add the following counters:
5. Click the **Add...** button in order to add some performance counters that we want to keep track of on this server.
6. Check the box for **Performance counter** and click **Next**.
7. Name your new Data Collector Set and choose the bottom radio button entitled **Create manually (Advanced)**. Then click **Next**.
   - **Processor** | **% Processor Time**: This will tell us how busy the CPU is.
   - **Memory** | **Available MBytes**: This will tell us how much RAM is available.
   - **Memory** | **Page Writes/sec**: This will tell us how often Windows looks to the paging file in order to create virtual memory, which helps to indicate whether or not the system is running out of physical memory.
8. As you can see, there are so many different counters that you can add. We are only interested in these three, and so we can click on the **OK** button:

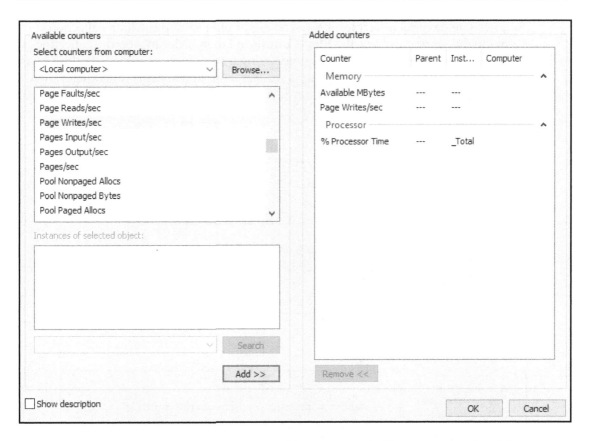

9. Back in our wizard for setting up the new Data Collector set, we should see our three counters now listed. Go ahead and click **Next**.

10. Change where you would like the data saved, if necessary. Then click **Next**.

11. On the last screen of the wizard, choose the radio button for **Open properties for this data collector set**. Then click the **Finish** button.

12. Navigate over to the **Schedule** tab and click the **Add** button to set your preferred time in the **Start time** field for these performance counters to be collected.

13. Once you have set a start time, you can either plan to stop the data collection manually, or you can use the **Stop Condition** tab in order to stop the collection after a predetermined amount of time. Using a combination of the **Schedule** and **Stop Condition** tabs is a great way to collect data for a specific time range, such as one day:

14. Now that we have some data that has been collected, head down to **Reports | User Defined** in order to see the data that was stored during the time period that we specified:

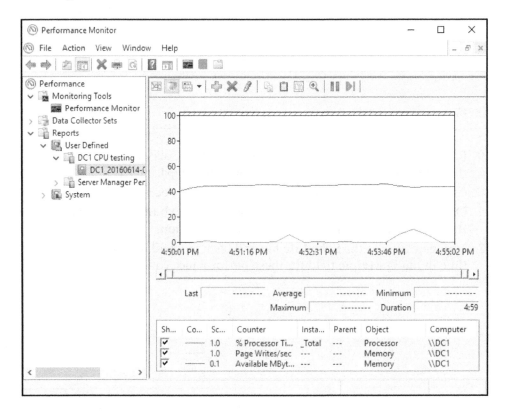

How it works...

Performance Monitor is a great tool for collecting hardware and server performance data. The ability to be very granular in identifying which resources you want to monitor is extremely helpful. Combine that with scheduling capabilities for collection times and you have a recipe for successful server monitoring. It can also be useful to run a Performance Monitor data set as a baseline after installing a new server. This way you can hold onto that report and compare it against later similar reports when the user load increases, to look back and find out what kind of an impact certain services or users have on a system.

Using Format-List to modify PowerShell data output

There is a special parameter that can be used with just about any PowerShell command or cmdlet in order to display different, and usually more, data from that particular command. This parameter is called **Format-List**, and if you are a fan of finding as much information as possible about the tools you are working with, this is something you will definitely want to become familiar with. PowerShell is often used to monitor many different facets of Windows Server, and getting to know the intricacies of Format-List will certainly help you to sculpt the output information that you are looking for when performing monitoring functions from the PowerShell command line.

We all know that a `dir` command will display a list of files and folders that are within our current directory; this works in either Command Prompt or in PowerShell. Let's start learning how to make use of Format-List by using it to modify the output of our `dir` information.

Getting ready

We will be running these commands from a PowerShell prompt on one of our Windows Server 2016 machines.

How to do it...

Let's use Format-List to modify our information output on a couple of different PowerShell cmdlets:

1. Open up PowerShell with administrative rights.
2. Browse to a location that contains some files. I have a few saved in my documents folder, so I will input cd documents in order to navigate into my documents folder.
3. Type dir. Then press *Enter*. You see the normal output of the dir command, a simple list of files, and a little bit of information about each of them:

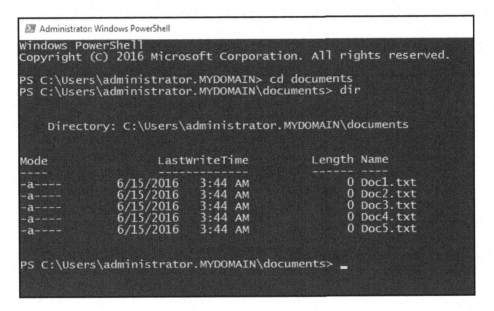

4. Now instead of using a simple dir, give this command a try: Dir | Format-List.

5. That is a lot more data! As you can see, by simply adding a pipe with Format-List following it, we have enhanced the `dir` command to give us more information about these files:

```
Name             : Doc5.txt
Length           : 0
CreationTime     : 6/15/2016  3:44:06 AM
LastWriteTime    : 6/15/2016  3:44:31 AM
LastAccessTime   : 6/15/2016  3:44:31 AM
Mode             : -a----
LinkType         :
Target           : {}
VersionInfo      : File:             C:\Users\administrator.MYDOMAIN\documents\Doc5.txt
                   InternalName:
                   OriginalFilename:
                   FileVersion:
                   FileDescription:
                   Product:
                   ProductVersion:
                   Debug:            False
                   Patched:          False
                   PreRelease:       False
                   PrivateBuild:     False
                   SpecialBuild:     False
                   Language:
```

6. Using Format-List by itself will adjust the data output to another default format, but one that contains more information. In order to see everything there is to see in the output of a particular command, you can also add a * to the end of the command. Let's give that a try.

7. Type this command: `Dir | Format-List *`.

8. Now we have yet another different output of information for these files:

```
Administrator: Windows PowerShell                                         —   □   ×

BaseName         : Doc5
Target           : {}
LinkType         :
Name             : Doc5.txt
Length           : 0
DirectoryName    : C:\Users\administrator.MYDOMAIN\documents
Directory        : C:\Users\administrator.MYDOMAIN\documents
IsReadOnly       : False
Exists           : True
FullName         : C:\Users\administrator.MYDOMAIN\documents\Doc5.txt
Extension        : .txt
CreationTime     : 6/15/2016  3:44:06 AM
CreationTimeUtc  : 6/15/2016  10:44:06 AM
LastAccessTime   : 6/15/2016  3:44:31 AM
LastAccessTimeUtc : 6/15/2016  10:44:31 AM
LastWriteTime    : 6/15/2016  3:44:31 AM
LastWriteTimeUtc : 6/15/2016  10:44:31 AM
Attributes       : Archive


PS C:\Users\administrator.MYDOMAIN\documents> _
```

9. Before we lay this one to rest, let's test Format-List with another cmdlet just to make sure this isn't something that only works with file information.

10. Use the `Get-Date` cmdlet to see the current date and time. Pretty simple, right?

```
Administrator: Windows PowerShell
PS C:\> Get-Date

Wednesday, June 15, 2016 4:49:08 AM

PS C:\>
```

11. Now try this: `Get-Date | Format-List`:

```
Administrator: Windows PowerShell
PS C:\> Get-Date | Format-List

DisplayHint : DateTime
Date        : 6/15/2016 12:00:00 AM
Day         : 15
DayOfWeek   : Wednesday
DayOfYear   : 167
Hour        : 4
Kind        : Local
Millisecond : 157
Minute      : 50
Month       : 6
Second      : 19
Ticks       : 636015630191577572
TimeOfDay   : 04:50:19.1577572
Year        : 2016
DateTime    : Wednesday, June 15, 2016 4:50:19 AM


PS C:\>
```

How it works...

As we have shown in this recipe, using the Format-List parameter on the end of any command or cmdlet is a good practice to get into because it can help display much more information than would normally be available with the original command, from system timestamps and file information up to very specific information about NIC settings and system components; making Format-List part of your regular arsenal will therefore help to get you a greater quantity of information that you can use to do your job.

Configuring a full system backup using Windows Server Backup

Maintaining a good backup solution is so critical to administering a corporate server environment in today's IT world. There are limitless potential options for designing your particular backup plan, all the way from file copy backups to redundant servers sitting in hot standby mode.

While many third-party tools and technologies provide the capability to back up all of your servers simultaneously while retaining multiple previous versions of each, those tools are not always on the table because of cost and implementation complexity. Let's take a few minutes and familiarize ourselves with the built-in backup solution that Microsoft provides free of charge, right in the Server 2016 operating system.

Getting ready

We are logged in to our Server 2016 web server. We will be using the built-in Windows Server Backup tool in order to create a full image of this server.

How to do it...

Follow these steps to back up your Server 2016 using the built-in Windows Server Backup:

1. Open **Server Manager** and click **Add roles and features.** Go through this wizard, following the steps in order to install the feature called **Windows Server Backup**. Remember that this is a Feature, not a Role, so look for it on the second screen.

2. Launch **Windows Server Backup** from your *Start* menu, or from the **Tools** menu inside Server Manager:

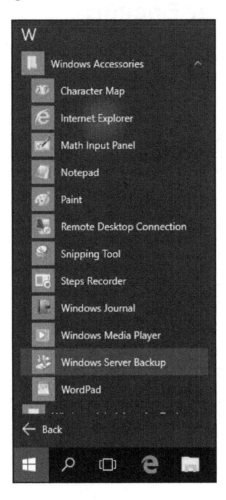

3. In the left window pane, choose **Local Backup**.
4. Then, toward the right of your screen, click on the **Backup Schedule...** action and click on **Next**.

5. On the **Select Backup Configuration** screen, I am going to choose **Full server**. If you have only specific items you would like to back up, you can use the **Custom** option for that purpose:

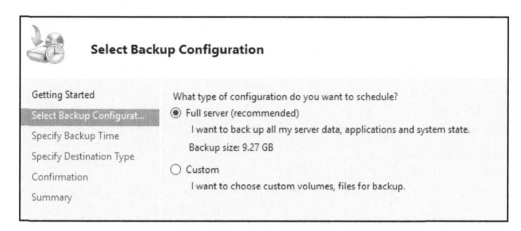

6. Specify the schedule for how often you would like these backups to run. I'm going to have mine run every morning at **2:00 AM**:

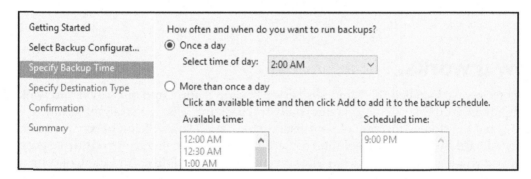

7. As you can see in the text, the best way to store backups is to have a dedicated hard disk plugged into your server. However, I don't have an extra drive installed here, so I am going to choose **Back up to a volume** and specify my D drive, a separate partition that has no data on it currently, as my storage container for backups:

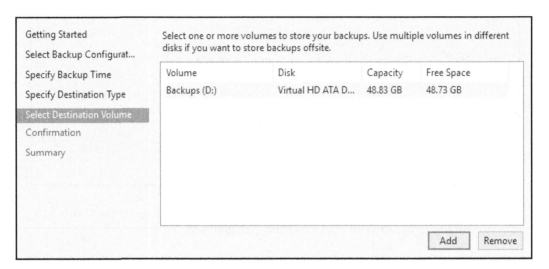

How it works...

In this recipe, we installed the Windows Server Backup feature into our server and walked through the wizard in order to schedule daily full backups. This is a straightforward process, but the storage location of your backup files can take a little bit of consideration. A dedicated hard disk is the best solution for storing backups; that way, if your drive goes down you will have all of the backup files on another physical disk. And then, of course, if you configure an option for replicating that data to another physical site, or rotating drives on a schedule, that will protect your data even better in the event of a site failure or catastrophe. Storing onto a separate volume on the same disk is also an option, but then you are in a situation where that physical disk is a single point of failure for both your live operating system and the backup files. The third option is storing backup files on the network. This is something that I expect a lot of admins will choose, but you have to keep in mind that, when making this configuration, you will only be able to have one backup file stored in that network location at a time from your server, as they will be overwritten with each new backup process.

There is a second action available from inside the backup console that we didn't touch on. In order to accomplish ad-hoc backups, or backups that you intend to create manually on an as-needed basis, you could launch an action called **Backup Once...** Use this to create a manual backup copy at any time.

Recovering data from a Windows backup file

Creating a backup or even a backup schedule is easy enough, but what is the process for restoring information from one of those backup files that we have sitting around? This is where the rubber really meets the road, as they say. Let's run through the process of restoring some data from a backup file that was taken yesterday. Perhaps some data was corrupted or accidentally deleted. Whatever the reason for our recovery needs, we will work together to restore some data from a backup file and get comfortable with that interface.

Getting ready

We are still working on our Server 2016 web server. This server was previously configured for Windows Server Backup, so it already has that feature installed. Yesterday we created a full backup of our server, and today we need to recover some of the data from that backup file.

How to do it...

Follow these steps in order to restore the server using the Windows Server Backup utility:

1. Open up the Windows Server Backup management interface. You can launch this from either the Start menu or from the **Tools** menu of Server Manager.
2. Choose **Local Backup** from the left window pane.
3. Near the right side of your screen, click on the **Recover...** action:

4. Since our backup file is stored right here on one of the server's volumes, we choose **This server** and click **Next**.

5. Now you will see a calendar with bold dates indicating which days have valid backup files that you can restore back to. We are selecting the backup that ran yesterday and clicking **Next**:

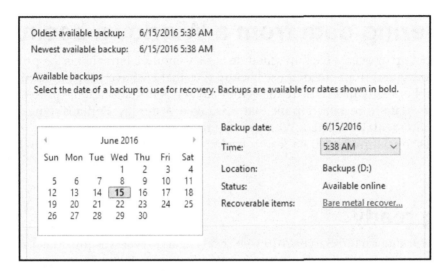

6. Now in the **Select Recovery Type** screen, we are going to choose **Files and folders** and click **Next**.

 You will notice a grayed out option here for Hyper-V. If you use Windows Server Backup on a Hyper-V server, you have options for backing up and restoring individual virtual machines on that host. This is a great feature enhancement and a good reason to start using Windows Server Backup on your Hyper-V servers.

7. We are now looking at the **Select Items to Recover** screen. Simply choose the files and folders that you want to restore from yesterday's backup. For our web server, which is the DirectAccess NLS server we set up a couple of chapters ago, it was the website itself that was compromised and we want to roll back to the website files that were running yesterday. So I am going to choose to restore the `C:\NLS` folder:

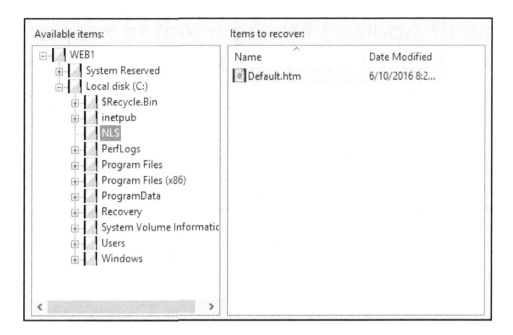

8. Choose the option to recover files to **Original location** and click **Overwrite the existing versions with the recovered versions**. This will ensure that the files from yesterday's backup get placed on top of the files that still exist on our server today.

9. On the **Confirmation** screen, you will see a summary of the items that are going to be recovered. If everything looks good, click on the **Recover** button.

How it works...

This recovery recipe is a good baseline for getting familiar with the options that are available to you for restoring from Windows backup files. Here we restored some simple files that had been compromised on our web server. In the event of a more serious system failure, where you might need to take a full disk backup and recover the whole thing onto a new server, that process is slightly more complicated. To accomplish a full system recovery of that magnitude, you would boot the server into your Windows setup disk and choose to run Windows Recovery Environment. Through this tool, you could make use of your Windows backup file and restore the server.

Using IP Address Management to keep track of your used IP addresses

The **IP Address Management** (**IPAM**) tool is a little-known utility built into Windows Server 2016. IPAM is a way that you can centrally monitor and manage some of the common infrastructure roles spread out around your network. Specifically for this recipe, we will be taking a look at IP addressing by using IPAM. Particularly in environments where there may be many different DHCP servers hosting different scopes spread out around your network, IPAM can be extremely useful for pulling all of that information into one management interface. This saves a lot of time and effort as opposed to launching the DHCP Manager console on each of your DHCP environments separately and trying to monitor them individually.

Getting ready

We have a domain network running that consists of all Server 2016 servers. Included in our network is a domain controller that is also serving as a DHCP server. We are adding a new server to this mix called IPAM1. This new server will be our IPAM management server, as the IPAM feature should not co-exist with either the AD DS Role or with the DHCP Role.

How to do it...

Let's take a look at our IP address utilization with the IPAM feature:

1. While logged in to the new server that you intend to use for IPAM, click the **Add roles and features** link from inside Server Manager.
2. Walk through this wizard, choosing the option to add the feature called **IP Address Management (IPAM) Server.**
3. Once the feature has been installed, you should see a new listing for IPAM in the left window pane of Server Manager. Go ahead and click there.
4. You will see that step 1 is already accomplished; the IPAM console is successfully connected to the local server. Go ahead and click on step 2 in order to provision the IPAM server:

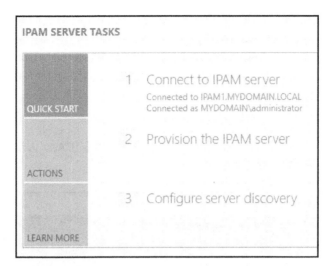

5. Click **Next**, after reading the information listed on that screen. As you can see, the best way to set up the interaction between the IPAM server and the infrastructure servers is to utilize Group Policy. We will define the settings for that on an upcoming screen in this wizard.

6. You should now be on the **Configure database** screen and we will leave the default option selected to utilize **Windows Internal Database (WID)**.

7. Now we get to select our provisioning method, which is where we are going to tell IPAM to use Group Policy in order to distribute the settings that it needs in order to manage and grab data from our infrastructure servers. Define a GPO prefix that is specific to this IPAM server:

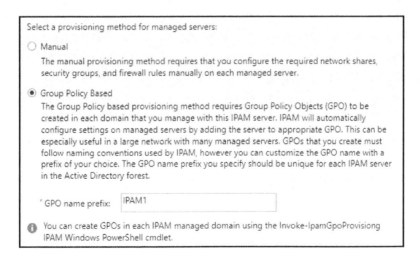

8. Before we complete this wizard, we need to take a special action in order to provision these GPOs so that the wizard can make use of them. To do this, we are going to use a PowerShell cmdlet. Open up PowerShell with administrative rights. Make sure you are logged into the server as a domain admin before running this cmdlet.

9. Type the following command into PowerShell: `Invoke-IpamGpoProvisioning`.

10. It will ask you to key in the name of your domain, as well as the GpoPrefixName. This is the same prefix that you just typed into the IPAM Wizard, so make sure you enter it exactly the same:

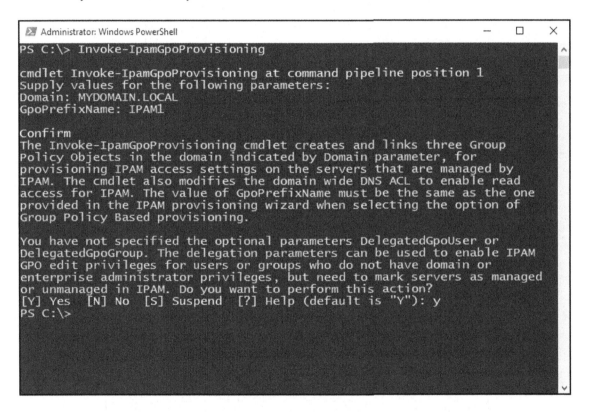

11. Now that our GPOs have been created, head back over to the IPAM Wizard and click the **Apply** button to finish it.

12. Now back at the IPAM section of Server Manager, click on step 3-**Configure server discovery**.

13. Use the **Add** button in order to query your domain for infrastructure services that can be monitored by IPAM. Select the roles you would like to pull data from (I am going to leave all three checked) and click the **OK** button:

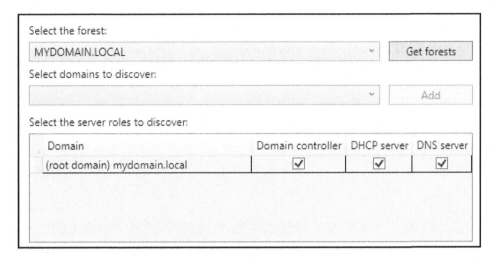

14. Click on step 4-**Start server discovery**. Wait for discovery to complete.
15. Click on step 5-**Select or add servers to manage and verify IPAM access**.
16. Right-click on the server that you want to collect data from and choose **Edit Server...**:

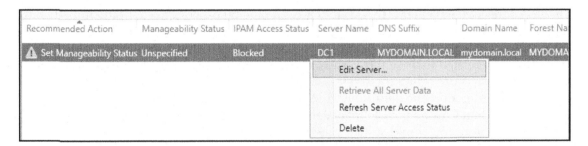

17. Change the server's **Manageability status** field to **Managed**.
18. Now head back to the main IPAM window in Server Manager and click on step 6-**Retrieve data from managed servers**.

You may have to wait for a little while to allow Group Policy to do its job in rolling out the settings.

19. Once data collection completes, you now have the ability to browse around inside the IPAM management console and view data about your DNS and DHCP infrastructure. For example, click on **IP Address Range Groups** to see a list of the DHCP scopes that are present on the DHCP servers that you are currently managing:

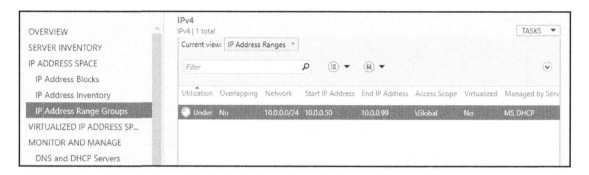

How it works...

The **IP Address Management (IPAM)** tool takes a little bit of work to configure initially but can be very beneficial later. Once configured to pull in data from your Domain Controllers, DNS servers, and DHCP servers, IPAM can be your one-stop-shop for monitoring and managing data related to these infrastructure roles. This is particularly helpful where you have many servers providing these roles, such as the case of multiple DHCP servers that each contain different scope definitions. In the past, you would have had to log in to each DHCP server or at least do remote management of them via Server Manager or some other tool, but ultimately you would still be viewing and managing the DHCP scopes individually. With IPAM, it brings all of this information into one place so that you can make decisions and configuration changes within your network while looking at the overall bigger picture.

Checking for viruses in Windows Server 2016

Monitoring and scanning for viruses on a Windows Server historically isn't a task that would have shown up in a book about the operating system, because in the past this functionality was always provided by third-party software. Starting with Windows 8, we got something called Windows Defender built into the operating system; this provided some semblance of free, built-in antivirus protection. Well, I'm excited to say that Windows Defender has continually improved over the past few years, and starting with Windows Server 2016, we finally have it available to us inside a Microsoft Server operating system! Installing third-party antivirus programs on servers has always been dangerous territory because they love to consume memory and cause random reboots. I've dealt with many different kinds of issues with antivirus programs on Windows Servers. Thankfully, Defender is baked right into the operating system, so we should never have to worry about those kinds of problems. Let's take a look at Windows Defender, which now comes standard as part of the Windows Server 2016 operating system.

Getting ready

Any Windows Server 2016 will do for this task, as Windows Defender exists on them by default. Today I happen to be using my WEB1 web server, and I want to make sure that Defender is turned on and protecting this system.

How to do it...

Follow these steps to look into the Windows Defender settings on your server:

1. From the **Start** menu, navigate to **Windows System | Windows Defender**.
2. Nice, this looks just like the Windows Defender that is provided inside my Windows 10 laptop, so it's familiar territory. From the Defender application you can see that I can update definition files, and run antivirus scans. You can also see that my definitions are currently out of date, oops! That is because my WEB1 server is inside an isolated test lab, and does not have access to the Internet:

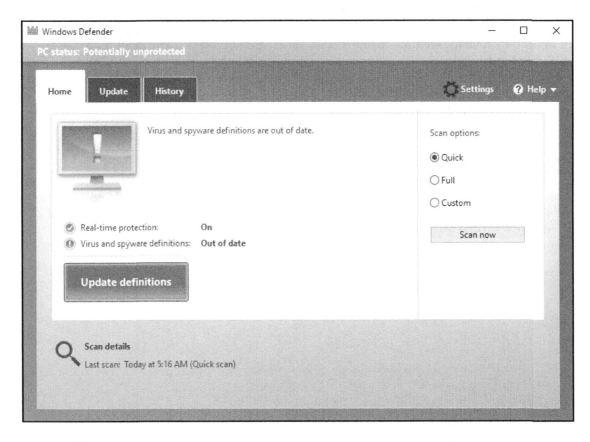

3. If you are paying attention, you will notice that there really aren't any settings in here about how Defender interacts with the operating system. In fact, there's not even a way to turn it off. To get into those settings, you need to open the Windows Defender section, available inside the Windows **Settings** menu itself. To get there, you can either click on **Settings** near the top-right corner of Windows Defender, or you can launch **Settings** from the Start menu. Let's take the Start menu approach.

4. Open the Start Menu and click on **Settings**.

5. Once inside **Settings**, click on **Update & Security**.

6. Now choose **Windows Defender**:

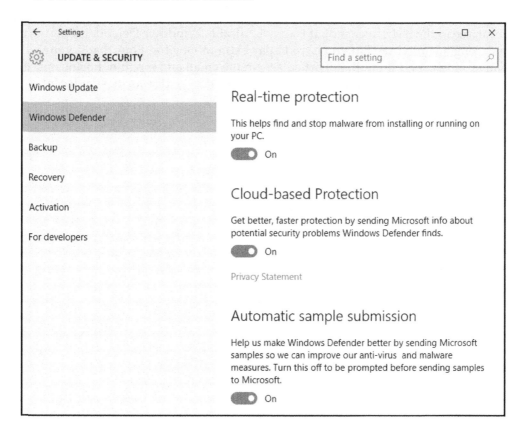

How it works...

I believe that having Windows Defender built into the Windows Server 2016 operating system is going to be a game-changer. The process of installing third-party antivirus software onto your servers is one of those things that always make admins cringe. You never really know whether or not it's going to play well with the server you have built. Now, I'm sure that many of you are not going to automatically trust Defender as an enterprise-ready and capable antivirus solution, but I believe that too will change over time. If it wasn't doing a good job, wouldn't Microsoft have thrown it away at this point, rather than continue to improve it and now trust it enough to exist inside a server operating system?

As you can see in the last screenshot, it is easy to disable Windows Defender if you want to continue using an antivirus that you have to pay extra money for. Fine, that is your prerogative. However, I think that, particularly in the small and medium businesses, this new inclusion is going to be incredibly useful from a safety and security standpoint.

6
Group Policy

In this book, we have already discussed a few recipes that call for the modification of **Group Policy Objects** (**GPOs**), but we have not taken the time to discuss why Group Policy is important in the first place. To those who have worked within Active Directory for a while, Group Policy may be familiar territory. I still find, though, that many IT folks working in the Server Administrator role are not overly familiar with Group Policy and how it can benefit them. Particularly in smaller companies, this incredibly powerful feature of Windows tends to be overlooked. It is easy to think of Active Directory as the storage container for your user and computer accounts because those are the core necessary tasks that it accomplishes. But as soon as you install the Domain Services role to configure your first Domain Controller, you have automatically included Group Policy capabilities into that domain.

Let's walk through some recipes together to make sure you are able to interact with Group Policy comfortably and begin to explore its underlying capabilities:

- Creating and assigning a new Group Policy Object
- Mapping network drives with Group Policy
- Redirecting the My Documents folder to a network share
- Creating a VPN connection with Group Policy
- Creating a printer connection with Group Policy
- Using Group Policy to enforce an Internet proxy server
- Viewing the settings currently enabled inside a GPO
- Viewing the GPOs currently assigned to a computer
- Backing up and restoring GPOs
- Plugging in ADMX and ADML templates

Introduction

Group Policy is a centralized administration tool for your domain joined systems. To summarize its capabilities, you can create policies in Active Directory, assign those policies to particular users or computers, and within those policies change any number of settings or configurations that are within the Windows operating system. The item inside Active Directory that contains these settings is called a Group Policy Object (GPO), so we will be focusing on the creation and manipulation of these in order to make some centralized management decisions that will affect large numbers of computers in our environment. GPOs can be utilized for user accounts, client computer settings, or for putting configurations onto your servers. Any domain joined system can be manipulated by a GPO, and typically settings put into place by GPOs cannot be overridden by users, making them a very integral part of security for companies familiar with making use of Group Policy regularly.

We will place a number of different configuration settings inside the GPOs that we create throughout this chapter, but we will not come close to covering even a fraction of the available settings that could be manipulated. For full coverage Group Policy settings that are available, please check out the following link: http://www.microsoft.com/en-us/download/details.aspx?id=25250.

Creating and assigning a new Group Policy Object

In order to start using Group Policy, we first need to create a Group Policy Object. Most commonly referred to as a GPO, this object contains the settings that we want to deploy. It also contains the information necessary for domain joined systems to know which machines and users get these settings and which ones do not. It is critical that you plan GPO assignment carefully. It is easy to create a policy that applies to every domain-joined system in your entire network but, depending on what settings you configure in that policy, this can be detrimental to some of your servers. Often I find that admins who are only somewhat familiar with Group Policy are making use of a built-in **GPO** called **Default Domain Policy**. This, by default, applies to everything in your network. Sometimes this is actually what you want to accomplish. Most of the time, it is not!

We are going to use this section to detail the process of creating a new GPO, and use some assignment sections called *Links* and *Security Filters*, which will give us complete control over which objects receive these systems, and more importantly, which do not.

Getting ready

Our work today will be accomplished from a Server 2016 domain controller server. If you are running the Domain Services role, you already have the items installed that are necessary to manage Group Policy.

How to do it...

Follow these steps to create and assign a new GPO:

1. Open **Server Manager,** click on the **Tools** menu and choose to open the **Group Policy Management** Console.

2. Expand your domain name and click on the folder called `Group Policy Objects`. This shows you a list of your current GPOs.

3. Right-click on the `Group Policy Objects` folder and click on **New**.

4. Insert a name for your `New GPO`. I am going to call mine `Map Network Drives`. We will end up using this GPO in a later recipe:

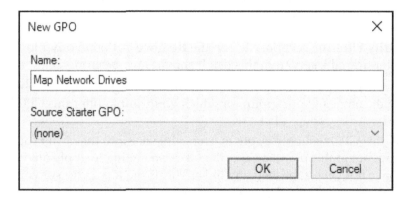

5. Click **OK**, and then expand your `Group Policy Objects` folder if it isn't already. You should see the new GPO on this list. Go ahead and click on the new GPO in order to see its settings.

6. We want this new GPO to apply only to a specific group of users that we have established. This assignment of the GPO is handled at the lowest level by the **Security Filtering** section, which you see on the following screen. You can see that, by default, **Authenticated Users** is in the list. This means that, if we created a link between this GPO and an **Organizational Unit (OU)** in the domain, the policy settings would immediately start applying to any user account:

7. Since we want to make absolutely sure that only specific user accounts get these drive mappings, we are going to modify the **Security Filtering** section and list only the user group that we have created to house these user accounts. Under the **Security Filtering** section, click on the **Remove** button in order to remove **Authenticated Users** from this list. It should now be empty.

8. Now click on the **Add...** button, also listed under the **Security Filtering** section.

9. Type the name of your group for which you want to filter this GPO. My group is called `Sales Group`. Click **OK**.

10. Now this GPO will only apply to users we place into the group called **Sales Group**, but at this point in time, the GPO isn't going to apply anywhere because we have not yet established any links. This is the top section of your **Scope** tab, which is currently blank:

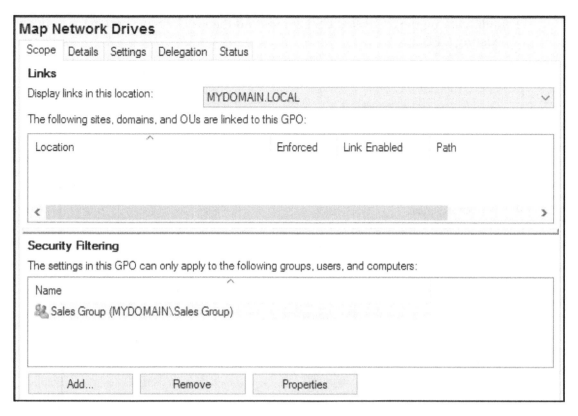

11. We need to link this GPO to some place in our domain structure. This is essentially telling it, *apply this policy from here down* in our OU structure. By creating a link with no security filtering, the GPO will apply to everything under that link. However, since we do have security filtering enabled and specified down to a particular group, the security filtering will be the final authority in saying that these GPO settings will only apply to members of our Sales group. For this Map Network Drives policy, we want it to apply to the OU called US Laptops.

12. Right-click on the OU called **US Laptops** and then click on the option for **Link an Existing GPO...**:

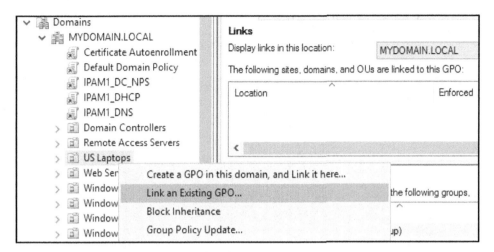

13. Choose the name of our new GPO, `Map Network Drives`, and click **OK**:

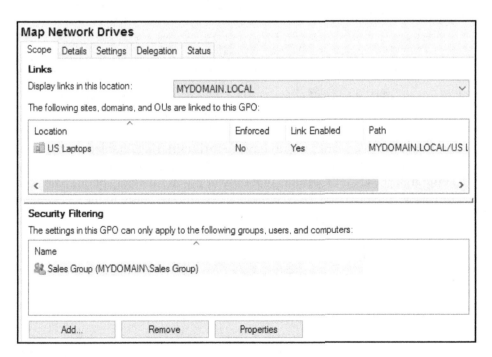

Our new GPO is now linked to the US Laptops OU, so at this level, any system placed inside that OU would get the settings if we hadn't paired it down a step further with the Security Filtering section. Since we populated this with only the name of our specific Sales Group, this means that this new drive mapping policy will only apply to those users added into this group.

How it works...

In our example recipe, we created a new Group Policy Object and took the necessary steps in order to restrict this GPO to the computers and users that we deemed necessary inside our domain. Each network is different, and you may find yourself relying only on the Links to keep GPOs sorted according to your needs, or you may need to enforce some combination of both Links and Security Filtering. In any case, whichever works best for you, make sure that you are confident in the configuration of these fields so that you can know beyond a shadow of a doubt where your GPO is being applied. You may have noticed that, in our recipe here, we didn't actually configure any settings inside the GPO, so at this point, it still isn't doing anything to those in the Sales Group. Continue reading to navigate the actual settings portion of Group Policy.

Mapping network drives with Group Policy

Almost everyone uses mapped drives of some flavor in their environments. Creating drive mappings manually as part of a new user start-up process is cumbersome and unnecessary. It is also work that will probably need to be duplicated as users move from one computer to another in the future. If we utilize Group Policy to centralize the creation of these drive mappings, we can ensure that the same users get the same drive mappings wherever they log into the network. Planned correctly, you can enable these mappings to appear on any domain-joined system across the network by the user simply logging in to the computer like they always do. This is a good, simple first task to accomplish within Group Policy to get our feet wet and to learn something that could turn out to be useful in your organization.

Getting ready

We are using a Server 2016 domain controller in our environment in order to create and configure this Group Policy Object. We will assume that you have already created a new GPO for this task that has been configured for Links and Security Filtering.

How to do it...

To create a drive mapping in Group Policy:

1. Open the **Group Policy Management** Console from the **Tools** menu of Server Manager.

2. Expand the name of your domain and then expand the `Group Policy Objects` folder. There we see our new GPO called `Map Network Drives`.

3. Right-click on the `Map Network Drives` GPO and click on **Edit...**:

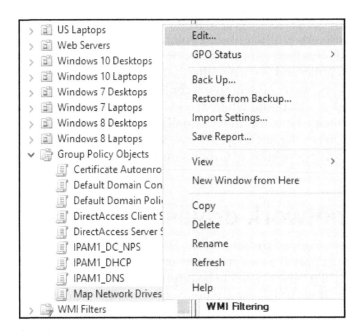

4. Navigate to `User Configuration | Preferences | Windows Settings | Drive Maps`.

5. Right-click on `Drive Maps` and choose **New** | **Mapped Drive**:

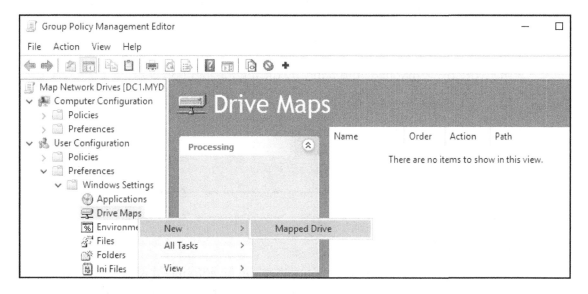

6. Set **Location** as the destination URL of the drive mapping, and use the **Label as** field if you want a more descriptive name to be visible to users.

7. Choose a **Drive Letter** to be used for this new mapping from the drop-down menu listed on this screen:

8. Click **OK**.

9. We are assuming you have already created the Links and Security Filtering appropriate to where you want this GPO to apply. If so, you may now log in to a computer on your domain as a user account to which this policy will apply. Once logged into the computer, open up File Explorer and you should see the new network drive mapped automatically during the login process:

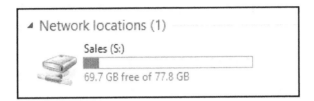

How it works...

There are a few different ways that drive mappings can be automated within a Windows environment, and our recipe today outlines one of the quickest ways to accomplish this task. By using Group Policy to automate the creation of our network drive mappings, we can centralize the administration of this task and remove the drive mapping creation load from our helpdesk processes.

Redirecting the My Documents folder to a network share

Users are accustomed to saving documents, pictures, and more into their Documents or My Documents folder because that is what they do at home. When working on an office computer at their job, the natural tendency is to save right into the local Documents folder as well. This is generally not desired behavior because backing up everyone's documents folders individually would be an administrative nightmare. So the common resolution to this problem is to provide everyone with mapped network drives and train users to save documents into these mapped drives. This is good in theory, but difficult to execute in practice. As long as users still have the capability to save documents into their local My Documents folder, there is a good chance that they will save at least some things in there, probably without realizing it.

This recipe is a quick Group Policy change that can be made so that the My Documents folders on your domain joined computers get redirected onto a network share. This way, if users do save a document into My Documents, that document gets written over to the file server where you have directed them.

Getting ready

We will set up our new GPO on a Server 2016 domain controller.

How to do it...

To redirect the My Documents folders via Group Policy, follow these steps:

1. Launch the **Group Policy Management** Console from the **Tools** menu of Server Manager.
2. Right-click on the name of your domain and choose **Create a GPO in this domain, and Link it here...**:

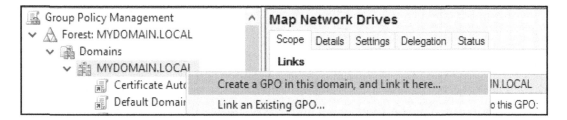

3. Input something in the **Name** field for your new GPO. I am going to call mine Redirect My Documents. Then click **OK**.
4. Browse to the Group Policy Objects folder that is listed under your domain name.
5. Right-click on the name of our new redirection GPO and click **Edit...**
6. Navigate to User Configuration | Policies | **Windows Settings** | **Folder Redirection** | Documents.

7. Right-click on Documents and go into **Properties**:

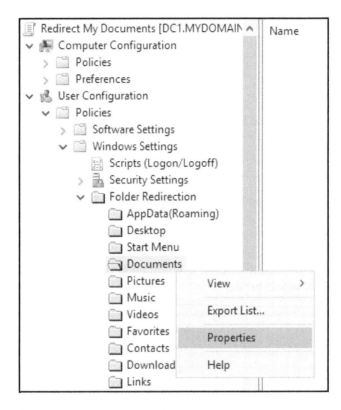

8. Drop down the **Settings** menu and choose **Basic - Redirect everyone's folder to the same location**.

9. Type in the **Root Path** field where you want everyone's `Documents` folder to be directed to. I am going to use a share that I have created on our file server. Mine will look like this: `\file1users`:

10. Click **OK**.
11. Your setting should be put immediately into place within the GPO. Now go ahead and log in to a test client machine and open up the `Documents` folder.
12. Create a new text document inside the local `Documents` folder. We are just creating something here in local `Documents` so that we can see where it is actually being stored.

13. Now log in to your file server and check inside the Users directory that we specified. We now have a folder in there with my username, and inside that folder is a Documents folder that contains the new text document that I just created and stored inside the local My Documents on my client computer!:

How it works...

Redirecting everyone's My Documents to be automatically stored on a centralized file server is an easy change with Group Policy. You could even combine this configuration with another that maps a network drive, then simply specify the drive letter in under your Document Redirection setting rather than typing out a UNC that could potentially change in the future. However you decide to configure it in your environment, I guarantee that using this setting will result in more centralized administration of your data and fewer lost files for your users.

Creating a VPN connection with Group Policy

If you have administered or helped support a VPN connectivity solution in the past, you are probably more than familiar with setting up VPN connection profiles on client computers. In an environment where VPN is utilized as the remote access solution, what I commonly observe is that the VPN profile creation process is usually a manual step that needs to be taken by human hands, following the user's first login to the computer. This is inefficient and easily forgotten. With tools existing in your Windows Server 2016, you can automate the creation of these VPN connections on the client computers. Let's use Group Policy to create these profiles for us during user login.

Getting ready

We will use a Server 2016 domain controller in order to configure our new Group Policy Object. Once finished, we will also use a Windows 10 client computer to log in and make sure that our VPN profile was successfully created. For this recipe, we are going to assume that you created the GPO and setup links, and filtered them according to your needs before getting started with the actual configuration of this GPO.

How to do it...

Follow these steps to configure a GPO that will automatically create a VPN connection profile on your remote client computers:

1. Inside the **Group Policy Management** Console, right-click on your new GPO that will be used for this task and click on **Edit...**
2. Navigate to `User Configuration | Preferences | Control Panel Settings`
3. Right-click on **Network Options** and choose **New | VPN Connection**:

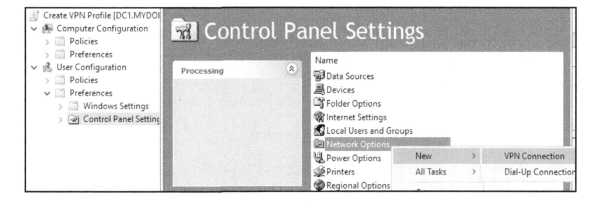

4. Input something in the **Connection name** field for this new VPN connection; this name will be displayed on client computers and the public **IP Address** field that client computers will need to connect to while working remotely. Depending on the needs for your particular VPN connection, you may also have to visit the additional tabs available on this screen to finish your specific configurations. Then click **OK**:

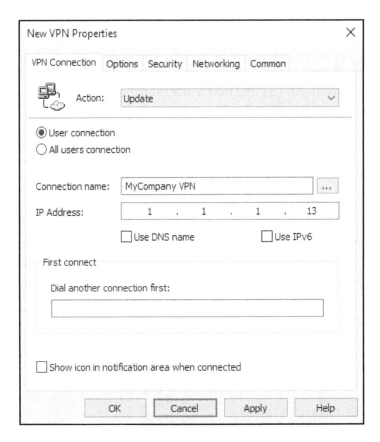

5. Now log in to your client computer and click on the Network icon in the systray, the same place where you would click in order to connect to a wireless network. You can see that, during our login to this computer, a new VPN connection called **MyCompany VPN** has been added and is now available to click on:

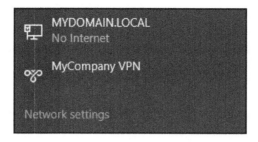

How it works...

In this recipe, we used Group Policy to automate the creation of a new VPN connection for our remote laptops. Using a GPO for something like this saves time and effort, since you are no longer setting up these connections by hand during a new PC build. You can also use this function to update settings on an existing VPN connection in the future, if you need to change IP addresses or something like that. As you are starting to see throughout these recipes, there are all kinds of different things that Group Policy can be used to accomplish.

Creating a printer connection with Group Policy

Let's say you just installed a new network printer in the office. You have installed it on a few computers to make sure it works properly, but now you are staring down the rows and rows of computers that would like to print to this printer occasionally. The prospect of logging in to every computer in order to launch and walk through the printer creation wizard isn't sounding like the way you would like to spend your Friday night. Let's see if we can once again make use of Group Policy to save the day. We will utilize a new GPO that will be configured to automatically install this new printer on the client desktops.

Getting ready

We are assuming you have already created the new GPO and have linked it accordingly so that only computers that need this new printer are going to receive these GPO settings. Now we are going to use Group Policy Management Console on our primary domain controller, which is running Windows Server 2016.

How to do it...

To configure your new GPO for a new printer creation, follow these steps:

1. Open **Group Policy Management** Console from the **Tools** menu of Server Manager.

2. Right-click on the new GPO that is going to be used for printer creation and click **Edit...**.

3. Navigate to `User Configuration` | `Preferences` | `Control Panel Settings`.

4. Right-click on **Printers** and choose **New** | **TCP/IP Printer**:

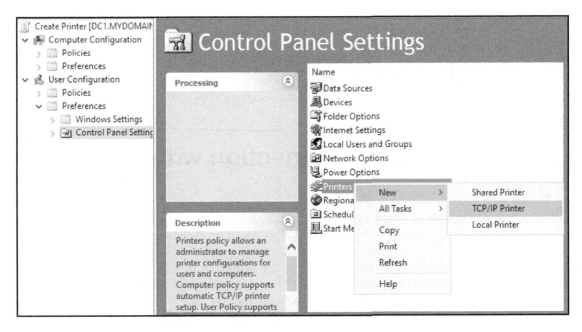

5. Input the information that is necessary for the printer connection. Since we chose to set up a new TCP/IP Printer, we need to input something in the **IP Address** and **Local Name** fields for users to be able to see this new printer in their list. I am also going to choose **Set this printer as the default printer... only if a local printer is not present**:

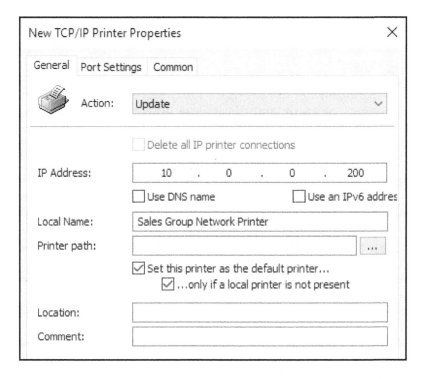

6. Click **OK**, and this printer will be distributed to those users you filtered the GPO to.

How it works...

Using Group Policy to automate regular IT tasks makes a lot of sense for all kinds of technologies. In this recipe, we built a simple printer connection so that we didn't have to do it by hand on our dozens of computers that needed the ability to be able to print here.

Using Group Policy to enforce an Internet proxy server

Most networks of significant size use a forward proxy server to filter their Internet traffic. This is essentially a box that sits out near the edge of the corporate network; whenever client computers in the network try to access the Internet, their requests are sent out through this server. Doing this enables companies to monitor Internet use, restrict browsing permissions, and keep many forms of malware at bay. When implementing a proxy server, one of the big questions is always "How do we enforce the use of this proxy?". Some solutions do a default route through the proxy server so that all traffic flows outbound that way at a network level. More often, though, it is desirable for the proxy server settings to be configured at the browser level because it is probably unnecessary for all traffic to flow through this proxy; only the browser's web traffic should do so. In these cases, you could certainly open up the Internet Explorer options on everyone's computers and enter the proxy server information, but that is a huge task to undertake, and it gives users the ability to remove those settings if they choose to.

By using Group Policy to set the Internet Explorer proxy configuration, this task will be automated and hands-off. This also ensures that users are not able to manipulate these fields in the future, and you can be assured that your web traffic is flowing through the proxy server as you have defined it.

Getting ready

Our GPO has already been created; now we are using the Group Policy Management Console on our Server 2016 domain controller to configure settings within the GPO. A Windows 10 client computer is also sitting waiting for use as we will want to test this GPO after we finish the configuration.

How to do it...

Follow these steps to set everyone's Internet proxy settings via Group Policy:

1. Open the **Group Policy Management** Console from the **Tools** menu of Server Manager.
2. Find the new GPO that you have created for this task, right-click on it, and choose **Edit...**

3. Navigate to User Configuration | Preferences | Control Panel Settings | Internet Settings.

4. Right-click on Internet Settings and choose **New** | **Internet Explorer 10**:

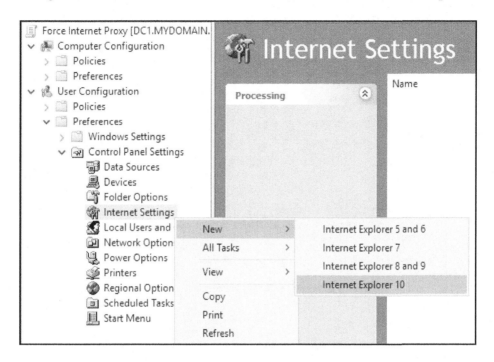

You may have to create multiple policies here if you are using multiple versions of Internet Explorer on your workstations.

5. You will see a dialog box that looks just like the regular Internet options available in IE. You have the ability to change many things here, but for our purposes today, we are heading over to the **Connections** tab.

6. Click on the **LAN settings** button.

7. Check the box for **Proxy server**. Then input the **Address** and **Port** fields for your particular proxy server:

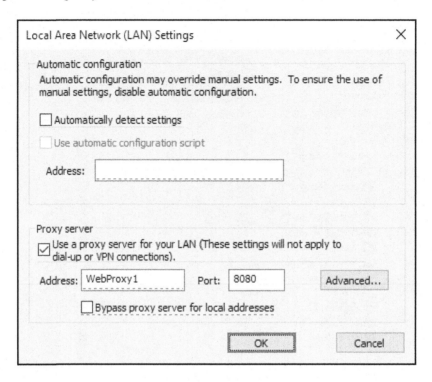

8. Click **OK**, and your setting will be put into place.
9. Now log in to the client computer, and let's see whether this proxy server information was successfully implemented. Launch Internet Explorer and open **Internet options**.
10. Browse to the **Connections** tab and click on the **LAN settings** button to ensure your proxy server settings have been properly plugged in. Also notice that they are now grayed out, showing you that they have been configured by Group Policy, and cannot be manipulated manually.

How it works...

Using Group Policy to assign Internet proxy server settings to all of your client computers with one simple GPO creation is another example of the power behind Group Policy. The possibilities for the centralized administration of your domain joined machines are almost endless; you just need to do a little digging and find the right place inside the GPOs for changing your settings. Maybe you don't have a proxy server in your network and don't need this recipe. But I still encourage you to take the steps listed here and apply them to some piece of technology that you do utilize. I guarantee anyone working in IT will find some setting inside Group Policy that will benefit them! Go out and find some that will help save you time and money.

Viewing the settings currently enabled inside a GPO

So far we have been creating GPOs and putting settings into them, so we are well aware of what is happening with each of our policies. Many times, though, you enter a new environment that contains a lot of existing policies, and you may need to figure out what is happening in those policies. I have had many cases where I install a new server, join it to the domain, and it breaks. It doesn't necessarily nosedive, but some component won't work properly or I can't flow network traffic to it for some reason. Something like that can be hard to track down. Since the issue seemed to happen during the domain join process, I suspect that some kind of policy from an existing GPO has been applied to my new server and is having a negative effect on it. Let's take a look inside Group Policy at the easiest way to display the settings that are contained within each GPO.

Getting ready

For this recipe, we only need access to the Group Policy Management Console, which I am going to run from my Server 2016 domain controller server.

How to do it...

To quickly view the settings contained within a GPO, follow these steps:

1. In the Domain Controller, open up Server Manager and launch the **Group Policy Management** Console from inside the **Tools** menu.

2. Expand the name of your domain, then expand the `Group Policy Objects` folder. This displays all of the GPOs currently configured in your domain.
3. Click on one of the GPOs so that you see the **Links** and **Security Filtering** sections in the right window pane.
4. Now click on the **Settings** tab near the top.
5. Once you have **Settings** tab open, click on the **show all** link near the top right. This will display all of the settings that are currently configured inside that GPO:

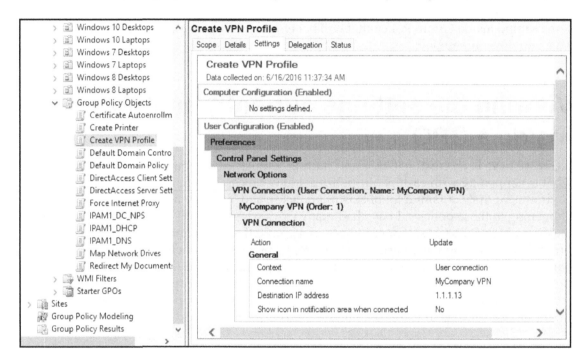

How it works...

In this very simple recipe, we use the Group Policy Management Console in order to view the currently configured settings inside our GPOs. This can be very useful for checking over existing settings and for comparing them against what is actually being configured on the client computers. Taking a look through this information can also help you to spot potential problems, such as duplicate settings spread across multiple GPOs.

See also

Viewing the settings included in a GPO can be helpful during troubleshooting, but there are many other tools that can be additionally used in order to troubleshoot Group Policy. Here are a couple of links to help you understand the recommended procedures for troubleshooting Group Policy:

- http://technet.microsoft.com/en-us/library/jj134223.aspx
- http://technet.microsoft.com/en-us/library/cc749336%28v=ws.10%29.aspx

Viewing the GPOs currently assigned to a computer

Once you start using Group Policy to distribute settings around to many client computers, it will quickly become important to be able to view the settings and policies that have or have not been applied to specific computers. Thankfully, there is a command built right into the Windows operating system to display this information. There are a number of different switches that can be used with this command, so let's explore some of the most common ones that I see used by server administrators.

Getting ready

We have a number of GPOs in our domain now; some are applied at the top level of the domain and some are only applied to specific OUs. We are going to run some commands on our Server 2016 web server in order to find out which GPOs have been applied to it and which have not.

How to do it...

Let's use the gpresult command to gather some information on policies applied to our server:

1. Log in to the web server, or whatever client computer you want to see these results on, and open up an administrative **Command Prompt**.

2. Type `gpresult /r` and press *Enter*. This displays all of the resultant data on which policies are applied, and are not applied, to our system. You can scroll through this information to get the data that you need:

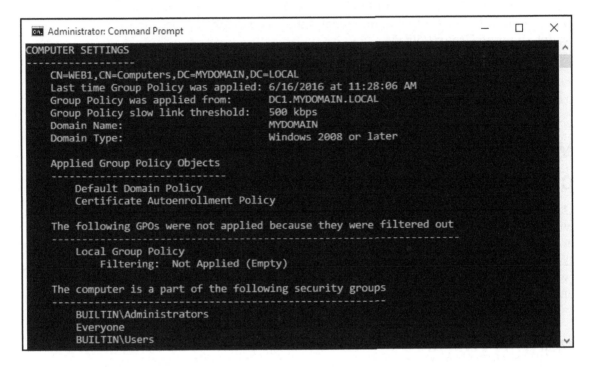

3. Now let's clean that data up a little bit. For instance, the general output we just received had information about both computer policies and user policies. Now we want to display only policies that have applied at the User level. Go ahead and use this command: `gpresult /r /scope:user`:

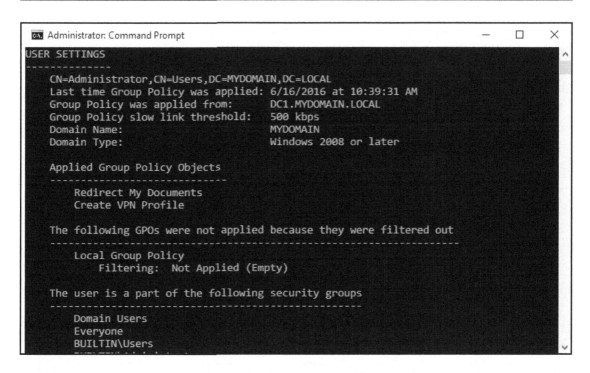

```
■ Administrator: Command Prompt                                    —    □    ×
USER SETTINGS
--------------
    CN=Administrator,CN=Users,DC=MYDOMAIN,DC=LOCAL
    Last time Group Policy was applied: 6/16/2016 at 10:39:31 AM
    Group Policy was applied from:      DC1.MYDOMAIN.LOCAL
    Group Policy slow link threshold:   500 kbps
    Domain Name:                        MYDOMAIN
    Domain Type:                        Windows 2008 or later

    Applied Group Policy Objects
    -----------------------------
        Redirect My Documents
        Create VPN Profile

    The following GPOs were not applied because they were filtered out
    ------------------------------------------------------------------
        Local Group Policy
            Filtering:  Not Applied (Empty)

    The user is a part of the following security groups
    ----------------------------------------------------
        Domain Users
        Everyone
        BUILTIN\Users
```

You can use either the /SCOPE:USER switch or the /SCOPE:COMPUTER switch in order to view specifically the user or computer policies applied to the system.

4. And if you aren't a huge fan of looking at this data via a command prompt, never fear! There is another switch that can be used to export this data to HTML format. Try the following command: gpresult /h c:\gpresult.html.

5. After running that command, browse to your `C:` drive and you should have a file sitting there called `gpresult.html`. Go ahead and open that file to see your gpresult data in a web browser with a nicer look and feel:

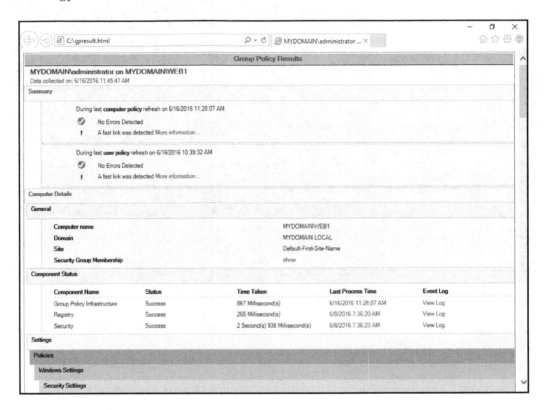

How it works...

The `gpresult` command can be used in a variety of ways to display information about which Group Policy Objects and settings have been applied to your client computer or server. This can be especially useful when trying to determine what policies are being applied, and maybe even more helpful when trying to figure out why a particular policy hasn't been applied. If a policy is denied because of rights or permissions, you will see it in this output. This likely indicates that you have something to adjust in your Links or Security Filtering in order to get the policy applied successfully to your machine. However you decide to make use of the data for yourself, make sure to play around with the `gpresult` command and get familiar with its results if you intend to administer your environment using Group Policy.

One additional note about another command that is very commonly used in the field. Windows domain joined machines only process Group Policy settings every once in a while; by default they will refresh their settings and look for new policy changes every 90 minutes. If you are creating or changing policies and notice that they have not yet been applied to your endpoint computers, you could hang out for a couple of hours and wait for those changes to be applied. If you want to speed up that process a little, you can log in to the endpoint client computer, server, or whatever it is that should receive the settings, and use the `gpupdate /force` command. This will force that computer to revisit Group Policy and apply any settings that have been configured for it. When we make changes in the field and don't want to spend a lot of time waiting around for replication to happen naturally, we often use `gpupdate /force` numerous times as we make changes and progress through testing.

See also

I tend to prefer `gpresult` to view the policies that are currently applied to a computer that I am working on, but it's not the only way. You may also want to check out `RSOP.MSC`. This is a tool that can be launched in order to see a more visually stimulating version of the policies and settings that are currently applied to your computer. Check out the details here:

- `http://technet.microsoft.com/en-us/library/cc772175.aspx`

Backing up and restoring GPOs

As with any piece of data in your organization, it is a good idea to keep backups of your GPOs. Keeping these backups separately from a full Domain Controller or full Active Directory backup can be advantageous, as it enables a quicker restore of individual GPOs in the event of an accidental deletion. Or perhaps you updated a GPO, but the change you made is now causing problems and you want to roll that policy back to make sure it is configured the way that it was yesterday. Whatever your reason for backing up and restoring GPOs, let's take a look at a couple of ways to accomplish each task. We will use the Group Policy Management Console to perform these functions, and will also figure out how to do the same backup and restores via PowerShell.

Getting ready

We are going to perform these tasks from a Windows Server 2016 domain controller in our environment. We will utilize both the Group Policy Management Console and the PowerShell command line.

How to do it...

There is a GPO in our domain called `Map Network Drives`. First, we will use Group Policy Management Console to back up and restore this GPO:

1. From the **Tools** menu of Server Manager, open up the **Group Policy Management** Console.
2. Navigate to **Forest** | **Domains** | **Your Domain Name** | **Group Policy Objects**.
3. If you want to back up a single GPO, you simply right-click on the specific GPO and choose **Back Up...** Otherwise, it is probably more useful for us to back up the whole set of GPOs. To accomplish that, right-click on the **Group Policy Objects** folder and then choose **Back Up All...**:

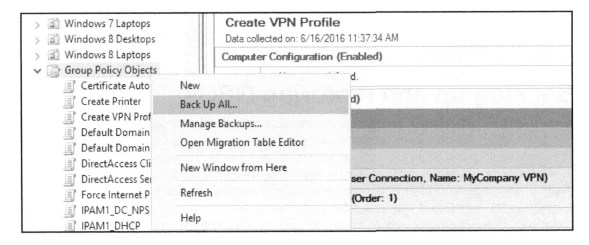

4. Specify a location where you want the backups to be saved and a description for the backup set. Then click **Back Up**:

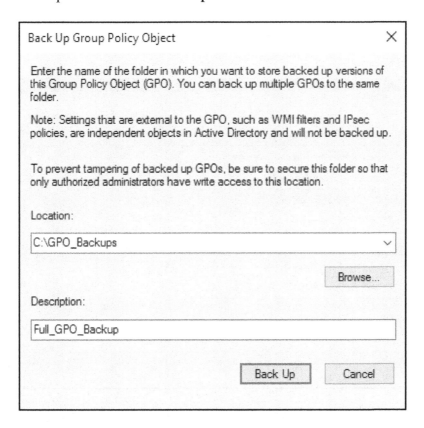

5. Once the backup process is complete, you should see the status of how many GPOs were successfully backed up:

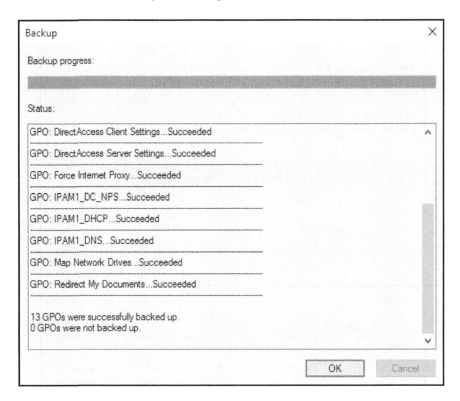

Now let's try accomplishing the same full GPO backup, but this time using PowerShell:

1. Open an administrative PowerShell prompt
2. Use the following command:

```
Backup-GPO -Path C:\GPO_Backups_PowerShell -All
```

Now that we have two full backup sets of the GPOs, let's try to restore the GPO called `Map Network Drives`.

1. Navigate back inside the **Group Policy Management** Console and find the `Group Policy Objects` folder. The same location that we used to back up a minute ago.

2. Right-click on the `Map Network Drives` GPO and choose **Restore from Backup...**:

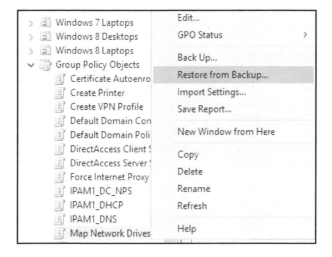

3. Click **Next** and specify the folder where your backup files are stored. Then click **Next** again.

4. As long as a backup copy of the Map Network Drives GPO exists in that folder, you will see it in the wizard. Select that GPO and click **Next**:

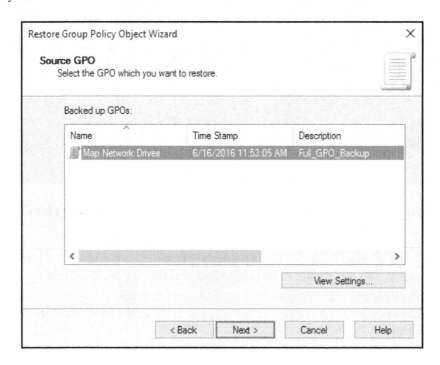

5. Click **Finish** and the GPO will be restored to its previous state.

Now we will restore the same Map Network Drives GPO, but using PowerShell as follows:

1. Head back to your administrative PowerShell prompt

2. Use the following command to restore the previous version of this GPO from the backup we created earlier:

```
Restore-GPO -Name "Map Network Drives" -Path
  C:\GPO_Backups_PowerShell
```

```
Administrator: Windows PowerShell                                    —   □   ×
PS C:\> Restore-GPO -Name "Map Network Drives" -Path C:\GPO_Backups_PowerShell

DisplayName        : Map Network Drives
DomainName         : MYDOMAIN.LOCAL
Owner              : MYDOMAIN\Domain Admins
Id                 : 77eed750-de8e-44e9-9649-96cab2f2abdc
GpoStatus          : AllSettingsEnabled
Description        :
CreationTime       : 6/16/2016 7:10:32 AM
ModificationTime   : 6/16/2016 11:58:58 AM
UserVersion        : AD Version: 2, SysVol Version: 2
ComputerVersion    : AD Version: 2, SysVol Version: 2
WmiFilter          :


PS C:\> _
```

Rather than typing out the name of the GPO in this command, you could instead specify the GUID of the policy. This number is generally a lot longer than the name, however, and so I tend to see admins preferring to utilize the name of the policy. For example, the GUID of our Map Network Drives GPO is 77eed750-de8e-44e9-9649-96cab2f2abdc.

How it works...

Backing up and restoring GPOs is going to be a regular task for anybody administering Active Directory and Group Policy. In this recipe, we walked through each process, using a couple of different tools for each procedure. Group Policy Management Console is nice because it is graphically interfaced, and it is easy to look at the options available to you. PowerShell is often preferred, however, because it can be automated (think scheduled backups). It also facilitates remote execution of these commands from another machine inside the network.

See also

Here are some links for more extensive information about the PowerShell cmdlets we used today:

- http://technet.microsoft.com/en-us/library/hh967480.aspx
- http://technet.microsoft.com/en-us/library/ee461030.aspx

Plugging in ADMX and ADML templates

Some day you may find yourself in a position where you are following a setup guide or some article, which instructs you to configure certain options inside a GPO. However, when you go to look for those options, they do not exist. How is that possible, if the documentation clearly shows the options existing inside Group Policy? This is the magic of ADMX and ADML files. Many configurations and settings exist inside Group Policy right out of the box, but some technologies build on additional settings or fields inside GPOs that do not exist by default. When this happens, those technologies will include files that can be placed onto your Domain Controller. These files are then imported automatically by Group Policy, and the settings will then appear in the normal GPO editing tools. The trickiest part about doing this is figuring out where the ADMX and ADML files need to reside in order for them to be seen and imported by Group Policy. Let's figure it out together.

Getting ready

I run across this one regularly when setting up DirectAccess. There is a special tool that you can install onto your Windows 7 computers that tells you some information about the DirectAccess connection, but this tool needs to be configured by a GPO. The problem is that the settings for the tool don't exist inside Group Policy by default. So Microsoft includes in the tool's download files an ADMX and an ADML file, both of which need to be plugged into Group Policy. We have downloaded this tool, called the DirectAccess Connectivity Assistant, and I have the ADMX and ADML files now sitting on the hard drive of my domain controller. The work we need to accomplish will be right from this DC1 domain controller.

How to do it...

In order to pull settings from an ADMX and ADML file into Group Policy, follow these steps:

1. Copy the ADMX file into `C:\Windows\PolicyDefinitions` on your domain controller. In my case, the filename is `DirectAccess_Connectivity_Assistant_2_0_GP.admx`.

2. Copy the ADML file into `C:\Windows\PolicyDefinitions\en-US` on your domain controller. In my case, the filename is `DirectAccess_Connectivity_Assistant_2_0_GP.adml`:

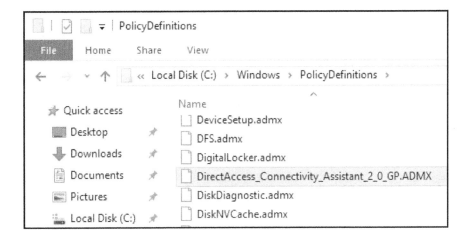

3. Now simply open your **Group Policy Management Console** from inside Server Manager.

4. Edit the GPO that you want to use with these new settings, and you can see that we have some brand new settings available to us inside here that did not exist five minutes ago! These new settings show up inside Computer Configuration | Policies | Administrative Templates:

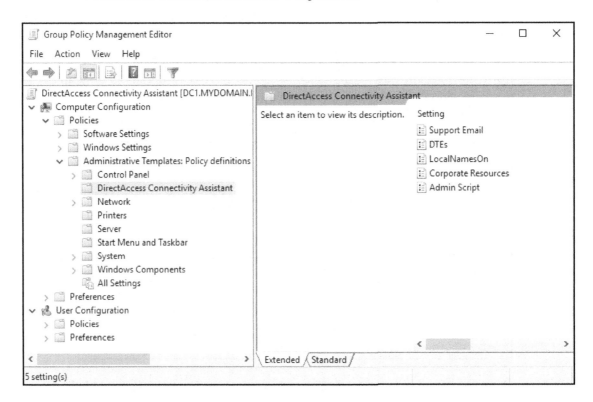

How it works...

You can import new settings and configuration options into Group Policy by taking ADMX and ADML files and putting them into the proper folders on your domain controller server. What we walked through today is an example of how to accomplish this task on a single domain controller, but what happens if your environment has multiple domain controllers? Do you have to copy the files onto each server? No, that is not the proper way to go about it. In an environment where you have multiple domain controllers, the ADMX and ADML files instead need to go inside something called the Active Directory Central Store. Instead of copying the ADMX and ADML files into their locations on the C drive, open up File Explorer and browse to `\<DOMAIN_NAME>SYSVOL<DOMAIN_NAME>PoliciesPolicyDefinitions`. This Central Store location will replicate to all of your domain controllers. Simply place the files here instead of on the local hard disk, and your new settings will then be available within the Group Policy console from any of your domain controllers.

Other Books You May Enjoy

If you enjoyed this book, you may be interested in these other books by Packt:

Windows Server 2016 Cookbook
Jordan Krause

ISBN: 978-1-78588-383-5

- Build the infrastructure required for a successful Windows network
- Navigate the new Server 2016 interface efficiently
- Implement solid networking and security practices into your Windows Server environment
- Design your own PKI and start issuing certificates today
- Explore the brand-new Nano Server functionality
- Enable nested virtualization on Hyper-V and Server
- Connect your remote laptops back to the corporate network using Microsoft's own remote access technologies, including DirectAccess
- Provide a centralized point for users to access applications and data by configuring Remote Desktop Services
- Compose optimal Group Policies
- Facilitate task automation with PowerShell 5.0 scripting

Windows Server 2016 Administration Fundamentals
Bekim Dauti

ISBN: 978-1-78862-656-9

- Become familiar with Windows Server OS concepts
- Learn how to install Windows Server 2016
- Learn how to install device drivers and run services in Windows Server 2016
- Learn how to add and install roles in Windows Server 2016
- Learn how to apply GPO to your Windows Server 2016 environment
- Learn how to tune, maintain, update, and troubleshoot Windows Server 2016
- Prepare for the MTA 98-365 exam

Leave a review - let other readers know what you think

Please share your thoughts on this book with others by leaving a review on the site that you bought it from. If you purchased the book from Amazon, please leave us an honest review on this book's Amazon page. This is vital so that other potential readers can see and use your unbiased opinion to make purchasing decisions, we can understand what our customers think about our products, and our authors can see your feedback on the title that they have worked with Packt to create. It will only take a few minutes of your time, but is valuable to other potential customers, our authors, and Packt. Thank you!

Index

W

21030137R00139